Two Cigarettes Coming Down the Boreen

To Keite
from Paul & Seas
Christmas 2014.

Hope you enjoy the read.

TWO CIGARETTES COMING DOWN THE BOREEN
Oral Narratives from a South Galway Community

Pauline Bermingham Scully
EDITOR

Pauline Bermingham Scully

ARLEN
HOUSE

Two Cigarettes Coming Down the Boreen

is published in 2015 by
ARLEN HOUSE
42 Grange Abbey Road
Baldoyle
Dublin 13
Ireland
Phone/Fax: 353 86 8207617
Email: arlenhouse@gmail.com
arlenhouse.blogspot.com

Distributed internationally by
SYRACUSE UNIVERSITY PRESS
621 Skytop Road, Suite 110
Syracuse, NY 13244–5290
Phone: 315–443–5534/Fax: 315–443–5545
Email: supress@syr.edu

978–1–85132–119–3, paperback

Typesetting ¦ Arlen House
Cover Image ¦ 'The Companions'
by Bernard Canavan
Oil on Canvas, 18 x 20in (2012)
reproduced by permission of the artist
courtesy of The Kenny Gallery, Galway

CONTENTS

To my beloved son Marcus
who sadly passed away in March 2005

ACKNOWLEDGMENTS

I gratefully acknowledge financial assistance from the NUI Galway Millenium Fund 2004–5 which helped in the taping and transcribing of these interviews.

I would like to acknowledge Caitríona Clear, lecturer in NUIG, who introduced me to Oral History.

Thanks to my many friends who have listened to me telling them stories about events that they didn't know what or who I was talking about.

My Mother, my daughter Meghann and my good friend Máire Holmes.

I thank the artist Bernard Canavan for his wonderful cover painting, and Dean Kelly at The Kenny Gallery, Galway for all his help with this.

Pauline Bermingham Scully

Two Cigarettes Coming Down the Boreen came about as a result of an oral history module which I undertook when doing a BA in NUI, Galway. This module was entitled 'Oral History and Personal Testimony'. The task was to interview an older person and I had difficulty selecting a person to interview. My first thought was my own mother who had been telling us stories about bygone days and memories of her own childhood. To my disappointment when I tried to interview her she could not recall anything of interest. My daughter Meghann also tried to interview her, but to no avail.

Betty Taylor was my next choice – a woman I had always admired, especially since as a child I was sent to buy milk as the Taylors had a small dairy. Betty lived in Ardrahan since 1939. I had known her all my life but I had never been in her home. I asked her grandniece to seek permission for me to interview; to my surprise Betty was delighted and it proved a great choice. She gave a wonderful insight into her life.

Betty's story gave me a fascination for oral history; I couldn't wait to finish college so I could begin collecting stories. Visiting one house directed me to another. A person might say to me 'Joe, Jack, Mary or Frank have great stories'. I could, more often than not, get a story out of them too. The story that I didn't expect to be good, was great, and where I was expecting a good story, I could be let down. It was a poignant experience to catch glimpses of a world that has all but vanished forever.

In the first half of the last century money was scarce. Water had to be drawn from a well or pump, if the village was lucky enough to have a supply. Most contributors recall when rural electrification came to the county. This consisted of one electric light in the kitchen. They had no electric appliances or mod cons. 'People wash themselves too much these days, they have all the natural oils washed away'. The men and women of Ardrahan and surrounding areas who tell their stories in these pages, are all rich in years and rich in experience. Their stories are from agricultural childhoods scarcely recognisable today.

The practice of helping one another was part of country and community life. This was highly valued. The tradition of *meitheal* meant neighbours gathered and worked for one another, on days when farm jobs needed many hands, such as threshing or saving the hay. The threshing day was one of the biggest days in the farming year. Most recall that when the work was done they celebrated the day by having a nice meal, prepared by the woman of the house. All the farmers' wives contributed to the meal by making cakes, bread, tart. The days often ended with a few songs or a bit of music played, and everyone went to bed with the knowledge that the corn was safe for that year. It was a time when people helped each other and there was an unbreakable social bond we don't see today.

The door of education was closed to many due to lack of money. Education was not considered important. It was out of the reach of the working classes. Some people didn't get the chance and left school at 13 or 14 having to earn. There were many mouths to feed so girls went into service. Some of these came from very big families.

Although several of these contributors have come to reside in the area of Ardrahan, the majority have lived here all their lives. A few of these people are well known to each other and some are related. Their stories not only shed light on individual lives, but the reader can build a picture of country life in South Galway from the 1930s up to the 1960s. In some of the homes I visited I was privileged by the welcome and excitement that people showed towards me when telling their stories. Others would recite songs or a poem that they learned in national school sixty years earlier. These recitations would be delivered without a hesitation or a stumble.

Some others shed a few tears, these would be tears of sadness and some tears of joy. This was normally when we spoke about a parent or sibling that has gone to their Maker. Some would have lost their mothers in childbirth, others died through neglect or not having the money to call the doctor. When I noticed a storyteller getting emotional we would stop the interview, take a break, have a cup of tea: we always returned to the interview. I was concerned not to leave anybody in an emotional state. What if they got upset when alone? I had awoken something that had been buried for years.

The interviews normally started with when and where people were born. I found this a gentle way to ease the storyteller into talking. Some were concerned that I was working for the taxman and others that they would lose their pension. I reassured everyone that this was oral history and that I had developed an interest in a collection of stories.

Times were tough; times were good; happy times. This is a statement that recurs again and again in these stories. To my surprise, no matter how painful a memory may have been, people were still happy having recalled it.

Thanks to all of you for sharing your stories with me and with future readers everywhere.

Two Cigarettes Coming Down the Boreen

DAN BERMINGHAM

Glasgow, 26 June 2003

Dan was born on 14 February 1917, in Coxtown, Ardrahan. There were 9 children in the family (12 births). His parents were Patrick Bermingham and Margaret Nolan from Ballyanna. He went to the old school in Labane, the teachers were Mr Flanagan and Bean Uí Fhathaigh [Mrs Fahy]. He left school at the age of 14. His first job was looking after a baby, Thomas Healy in Rahealy. He nursed him from the day he was born. His father got £6 for six months. His next job was clerk in the parish church in Labane. Fr. Considine brought him to Coens in Gort and rigged him out in a new suit, collar and tie. They fell out after six months, so when the clerk's collection came around at the end of the year, Fr. Considine took the price of the suit out of the collection and gave the rest of the money to Dan's father.

17

His next job was with Roches in Gort. He served his time there as a mechanic. He loved Roches, 'a wonderful time'. He started driving, bringing crowds to dances in Loughrea, 'plenty of women'. After leaving Roches he went driving for Maggie Shaughnessy in Kinvara, 'she is no longer there'; they had a hackney that was: a fantastic time altogether, we used to meet the tenders coming in from America, the boats coming in from America, a tender in Galway would pick up the Yanks, we would meet the tenders, that was yours for a fortnight, you could get a watch, that was a great time.

I got sacked from there Christmas Eve. We went to Loughrea. I had a load from Kinvara and Andy Quinn had a load from Labane. We met in the pub after Mass. We had a load of pints, we made a bet who would be in Labane first. I went by Craughwell – he went some other way. The next morning there was a funeral in Kinvara. I was under the weather. I fell asleep behind the wheel and hit the hearse – Paddy Lally.

I left for England in 1937, my mother drove me to Ardrahan in an ass and cart. I was going to inherit from my uncle in Ardrahan. I was to be heir to the throne, but I got the bullet.

There was nothing, absolutely nothing around. A Greally man from Clarinbridge was going to England so I went with him. We went to Wimbledon. I got a job digging a big hole. I wasn't fit for it, my hand were cut. The ganger said to me, 'have you done this work before?' When I told him I hadn't, he sent me to the Labour Exchange to get a juvenile card and gave me the job making the tea.

Then he got a job in the Prince of Wales Hotel in Wimbledon. When the war broke Dan decided to leave England. There was an excursion to an All-Ireland Final for twelve shilling and six pence from the hotel, so Dan took this. When he arrived in Dublin he met his brother Miko off the train. He had two sisters working in Dun Laoghaire. He stayed with them and got a job as a chauffeur. He wasn't long at home when he got itchy feet. He saw an advertisement in the Connacht Tribune – McAlpine was looking for men for the war effort. He went to Loughrea for an interview. His fare was paid to Holyhead. At Holyhead there was a man standing at the bottom of the gangway saying 'Scunthorpe or Girvan'. When it came to his turn he asked where was Scunthorpe? He was told England, and then asked where was Girvan and was told it was in Scotland.

Oh to hell, I was in England before, so I'll go to Scotland, that's how I ended up in Scotland. That was in 1940.

In Loving Memory of
TOM BERMINGHAM
Shrove, Ardrahan,
Co. Galway,
who died on 26th November, 2005,
aged 82 years.
Rest in Peace.

*He was born in Castletaylor in 1923 with two in his family.
He went to Kiltiernan NS. His teachers were Mr and Mrs
Burns.*

I was a poor scholar. I got a sickness when I was nine
years old. Diphtheria, and I got it doubly. My brother
got it too, very lucky to live, it wasn't expected. 'Twas
a terrible time. Dr Sexton was in Ardrahan that time.

Thank God I pulled through, I did. I kept going to school until I was fourteen.

There were any amount of families in Castletaylor at that time, three Bermingham families, Burns are gone, Conoles are gone, Burkes are gone, Glynns, Stankards are gone, an awful lot of new houses. There was a big family of Mantos. O'Neill's, Guilfoyles, Tierneys are gone. Mick Martyn and wife are gone. There was a terribly big population one time. Bad times – there are great times now. Shaw-Taylor was a fine man; if he got one lie off you, he would never ask to see you again. He had racehorses one time, in the early '40s the races were everywhere – Galway. There were races in Ardrahan – Tarpey's field, local lads used to ride in them. I remember your father, the Lord have Mercy on him.

Tom recited a poem about his home-place:

'Castletaylor Grove'

Mary Keighrey

I am going to take a last fond look at Castletaylor Grove,
And on those dear and lonely paths that we have known of
old.
There is not in this wide world today a dearer spot to me,
Than a fairy dale that lies hidden there by trees and
evergreens.

I walked beside the castle grand, its shrubberies and lawn,
To view the primroses so sweet the daffodils and all.
The grand and towering beeches, there standing on each
side,
While the holly grows and clusters there the little birds to
hide.

The lone old road that leads to it by every root and tree,
Reminds me of the good old days when we were young
and free.
It's many the pleasant ramble with comrades young and
gay,
They are scattered now both far and wide beyond the
distant sea.

Alas some of them lie buried there that never forgot will be,
By one lone heart who is striving now its sorrows to
conceal.
So fare thee well to our fond comrades, to our rambles long
ago,
To Boreen Glass and the Wellpark Gate and the stile we all
well know.

To the corner too where Burke was shot and the ivy covered
wall,
How often have we rambled there to count the portholes all.
On a summer Sunday evening with hearts too light and
gay,
Those dear old days, those good old days they were too
good to stay.

Could anything look grander than those hedges all around,
The hawthorn and the Gossamer so very neatly bound.
But no matter where I wander to or no matter where I roam,
My thoughts will always travel back to those scenes around
my home.

24 June 2003

I was born here in Deerpark in 1915. There were five girls and myself. My parents were Michael and Nora. There were two of my sisters joined the nuns, and there's three of them got married – one in Gort, Mrs Hayes, and one was married to Paddy Hamrock in Lough Cutra, and the other girl was married in Tubber, she died young. She was married to Michael O' Grady.

The name Deerpark came from the time of the landlords, they owned this place. It was a deerpark, for the people that was living out there in the castle.

There was no radios that time, no television, and all the neighbours would visit each other, and that'd be the conversation. The cricket would be brought in before the conversation would be over, and I used to love to be listening to them. They had a cricket team down in Coole that time, all the neighbours, the tenants used to play in it, and they'd give them a ball once a year, four or five half-barrels of Guinness, they used to have a – that was for the tenants now, they used to have an awful good time, a great time.

I met Lady Gregory, we used to meet her at the school, sure when she'd come down with apples. She'd come once a year, once a year. And I remember to see her going into church, in Gort, in a horse and carriage, and John Diviney'd be driving her. He had a tall hat, he couldn't look at anybody. She was the most popular woman in the world around this area, Gort, she was, she was a lovely lady. I went in to Coole, once, I went in with my uncle one time, he went in for some timber or something, and we met her at the hall door. She'd talk to me and she'd give me half a crown. Now she was a lovely lady. She loved the people of Kiltartan, and Gort. She did. She was an awful popular lady.

PAULINE: *And used you go up to Thoor Ballylee?*

No, but William Butler Yeats used to come down across to Coole. We often met him on the path, mass-path, often. I often met him. He'd never speak to you at all. He'd be standing up listening, we thought he was crazy, he'd be going along, then he'd stand up and he'd be listening for about five minutes, and then he'd be off again. Oh he was a real genius, sure, genius, but like he usen't bother with anybody. He used have an Irish wolfhound, most times, walking with him. But he used to go down regular to Lady

Gregory, so he would. And you'd see them walking up and down across the fields; there was mass-paths that time in every village you could say, to school, and Mass, and he used to come down that way, but he wouldn't talk to anyone. When we were children we thought Coole was the greatest place on earth, we heard so much about the Gregorys and everything and all the big people calling there, the poets and writers, their names are all on a tree there ...

'Twas the Gregorys built the Kiltartan school, the man that built it lived over here in Ballylee, Martin Leenane was his name. He lived there within a hundred yards of Thoor Ballylee. He had a mill, he used to cut timber, grind corn, lots of jobs like that, but he was a big rough man, not an over-exact man, mighty strong.

Lady Gregory died in 1932, the monument is still there, Sir William, and then she had a son, Master Robert. He was killed in the war. There was two daughters that were reared then in Coole, Miss Anne and Miss Catherine. They were two lovely girls, wild, but lovely girls. They used to come to the school with the old lady, when she'd come with the apples. That was the only time I met them, now. They kept on their own, I tell you. They didn't mix at all much.

My first job when I left school was farming, farming. I had the farm here. You might think it's a lovely spot? It is now, but one time it was very lonesome in here, no cars, bad road, things improved all right. I got married in 1947. I met herself at a dance in Labane. That's fifty-five years now, we had our fiftieth anniversary, there was eleven cars outside the house that evening, there was a Mass in Kiltartan and we had a do after that, we had all the neighbours.

In 1932 myself and Jack Fahy we went to the Eucharistic Congress, we did, and 'twas a sight. He told me when we came to the gate of the Phoenix Park; look in there, he said, you'll never see the like of that again. A quarter of a million people, 'twas nothing but a sea of heads, that was the year Lady Gregory died.

Sir William was old, I'd say, when he got married. But they were very popular people, so they were. And the Persses – she was Persse, from Roxborough – they weren't that popular, now. They weren't so nice to the tenants, now. But she was – out on her own. Oh she was. Very generous and everything, and sure she was. She was an awful clever lady, sure she wrote plays. Coole House was vacant for a good few years there and everyone was going in it, wrecking it, that's what was happening, people didn't appreciate it at all. And there'd be a college one time there only that Archdeacon Cassidy, he objected, he said 'twould be a wrong place to have youngsters going in around the woods. 'Twould have been lovely. There could be a lovely hotel in it, that's a fact. People were slack around that time, that somebody didn't buy it, could be bought cheap you know.

PAULINE: *Do you see a lot of change in the place nowaday?*

Oh *[emphasis]* a lot of changes.

PAULINE: *For good or bad?*

For good of course! When I was growing up 'twas slavery, we had to do everything the hard way. 'Tis all done sitting down now, tractors and machinery, 'tis the truth, but when we were growing up, saving hay and forking rake, that's what we did. There's an awful change, change for the better. Sure the young lads don't know how to catch a fork or a rake now. But that bloody thing there [*the television*] and the radio, people now, they don't mix, they don't even know their cousins, they don't know their *first* cousins would you believe that, the young lads wouldn't be bothered, they never talk about relations or friends, the old people would be always talking about their relations.

DESMOND COEN

18 March 2004

I was born in Bridge Street over our store in April 1921.
I lived there for 70 years and moved when I retired. My
father was John J. Coen and my mother was Aideen
Coen, nee Kenny, she was from Caher, Co. Clare. They
ran a drapery shop in Bridge Street. We had another
one across the road where we did ladies' fashion. My
grandfather was in business in Bridge Street, he was in
the hardware business. When my father came of age he

said 'What would you like to do?' and he [*my father*] said 'go into the drapery business'. He went into Moons in Galway, did his time there, for three years during the '14–18 war. Then he came out and started up in Gort on Easter Saturday morning 1916 at 9 o'clock in the morning, and at 12 o'clock he was in Galway jail. He was a member of the IRB and all the boys were rounded up and brought to jail. His first week in business in Galway jail! A fairly dramatic opening. When I was born in 1921 my father was on the run, my mother had to flee to a – not the workhouse – there was a Fever Hospital up there near George Daly's. The nuns took her in and myself for shelter, we spent a week there. In the meantime the shop was raided by the military and a lot of the stock was taken.

I had two brothers and one sister, one of my brothers is dead and the other one lives in London. I went to the local school in Gort, then I was sent away to a boarding school in Thurles at the age of 12 and after that I went to Mount St. Joseph's in Roscrea, then I came home and started in the business. I got married in 1948 and still lived over the shop. My father moved out to Church Street. We were very successful, the country people were great to support us, people shopped at home in those days – now they want to travel.

It was pretty hard to get stuff during the war years – but we had some decent suppliers who looked after us and we always had a fair sprinkling of goods. Farmers were easy enough to please, anything that suited them at all in the line of working clothes and nailed boots. Then they got very scarce and we had to turn to clogs with wooden soles. There was a lot of clogs sold during the war, they didn't require much leather. There was a couple of factories – one up in Westport making clogs.

PAULINE: *I thought clogs were a new thing.*

There was a lot of clogs, they wouldn't bend at all with the wooden sole, clattering along. We sold a lot of clogs during the war and the controlled price was stamped on to the sole so you couldn't overcharge. They came from the manufacturers and you were allowed a profit of 33.3%, so that was generous enough.

PAULINE: *Do you know anything about Lady Gregory?*

My first memory of Lady Gregory was when our housekeeper took my brother and myself for our usual walk, he was in the pram. I was walking beside just as you go up to the railway station, a carriage came down and John Diviney was the man sitting up in his box with his tall silk hat. He had just met Lady Gregory off the 7 o'clock train and brought her back to Coole – probably up at the Abbey Theatre in Dublin which was in its infancy in those days. Another thing I remember as a child, playing up here at the Church of Ireland where the local gentry came each Sunday to service and we used to play around the carriages, traps and all that. We could see them going in and coming out from service and there were two galleries in the Church, one was for the Gregorys and the other for the Goughs of Lough Cutra – facing one another and the general body for the rest of the people. It is now the library, a beautiful building – then in years later when I came home from school in the summer time we used to camp down in Coole near the horse pump, and we used to swim in the river there before I came into work. There wasn't a soul in Coole in those days, only the forester, it was lovely. She was gone by then.

Another funny story – this man came into the shop to my father about 1940, he got talking to him. He said he was in charge of the demolition of Coole House. My father was horrified to hear this and he said you will regret this some day. I had great association with Coole all down through the years. I used to ramble around the woods there. I love to go down and have a walk there. We are so lucky to have it. People don't use it enough. People are coming from far and wide to see it.

PAULINE: *Could you tell me a little bit about the Coen family?*

My grandfather was born in Kilbeacanty and he came into Gort as a young man after leaving Kilbeacanty National School. He was apprentice to Glynns hardware, now the AIB Bank, he worked there for some years, eventually he was the charge-hand there and the Glynns depended on him an awful lot to run the business for them. Then he decided to set up on his own. He bought a small place in Bridge Street and the Glynns were very annoyed with him because they didn't want to lose him. They fell out with him. In a few years they got over it and Sir Joseph Glynn who, I think afterwards had a big post in Australia, I think, Governor-General, he was seen on a few occasions inside the counter with a big sheet over him and my grandfather cutting his hair. He prospered and he bought next door to where he was from Sheehans and that's where my father set up in the drapery business and then grandfather bought another shop across the road from a family of Hunters. They were Scotsmen – imagine Scotsmen living in Gort in the drapery business in those days.

PAULINE: *Did the Hunters leave Gort?*

They were two old men and one of them could be seen in through the window combing his beard – I don't know why I am telling you this! Grandfather went down then and bought Raheen estate which was owned by the O'Hara family. The grandfather and grandmother had, I think, six sons and one daughter, one son was killed off a motorbike going out to

Spiddal and another died very young too, and two emigrated to America. When the one died off the motorbike, one was sent for, that was Bernard, and he came home and built up a great business there. It is only in recent years his son sold it and we ourselves have just sold our store – you saw it being demolished.

PAULINE: *Have you seen a big change in Gort down through the years?*

O yes – when I started in business first in 1936 there were very few motorcars and the farmers came in in their horse and cars, donkey and cars and traps and bicycles – nothing for them to do – fool around all day – no running home. It was a pleasure dealing with them because they were great people – great loyalty.

PAULINE: *You must have seen a lot of poverty as well.*

Yes, well, farmers did alright, they were able to pay their way.

PAULINE: *Used you run a book?*

O yes and we have some tales still in the book. The grandfather had a pub next door and he used to get a hogshead of whiskey, I think it was somewhere in the region of 60% proof gallons, from Persses Distillery in Galway. It used to come by train to Athenry to Gort and he would send a couple of men up to the train to unload it. It was a big barrel, bring it down on to the horse car through the archway down in the yard. They would bucket water from the river to thin out the whiskey, to bring it down to the right proof. Let's say it was 80 proof, they had to bring it down to 30, that was sold then in gallon jars, the stone crocks. They would use it for wakes and parties, marriage parties.

When a person died out the country they would come in to get a couple of gallons of whiskey, a barrel or two of Guinness, a case of clay pipes and a big round of tobacco.

You would have to loan them the knife – there was a special knife for cutting it – and you might get paid for it in a year's time, when they sell the cattle – yes indeed.

28 October 2003

This house was built in the 1870s because – my forefathers were buried in Kilmacduagh, because there's a graveyard marked there in 1803, so it had to be the 1870s then, here. There was stones in a quarry down in Blackrock there, it's all stone building, it still is a thatched house. I still live there. I am the fifteenth generation of Coens living in that house. The Coens are one of the most ancient families in south Galway. That is the history of the house, now. But down the back then, there was more history attached to it, prior to the land, dating from ... The old cross in Ardrahan was taken from this land, the stones from the base of the cross were shown by an old man, Pat Shaughnessy. The stones are still there, but that land has been sold three times since then and the present crowd wouldn't know the history at all of it. At that time, it being outside the wall, I saw the long stone, the foundation stone that was never taken out of it. The history of that stone, on top of that stone, was a spike or a nail, there was a spike – a nail they called it – before any solicitors' offices or any writing and it was there 'at that Cross under that nail' any bargain was made it was said then that the deal was made 'under the nail'. Ardrahan came into prominence after that, whenever it was, but alongside of that old Cross adjacent to my land there was a wall built there, a massive wall of between six and seven feet high, it seemed to be one of the old villages of bygone times.

PAULINE: *You were telling me the last day about the fairy tree?*

There's a field very near that, second field from it, it's in a hollow, and it was ever called Tobar a'Chaimín, that'd be the crooked well in English, and in that field in the little hollow there was a bush that grew up and it was said that it was a blessed well, and a local lady came for water to the blessed well, to water her cow, and the well closed in. Well I've seen that tree, in my young days, up to 19 – what year we had [*Hurricane*] Debbie, '61 was it, it was knocked. Well it flooded now and again. I had lambs there and I was afraid they would get drowned, so I went in under the tree to release the water. It was about 2 feet, I had a crowbar about 6ft long – this is a fact now. I tried to – I drove it down where the land was soft, and the next thing the crowbar all but went off my hands, so it must be open underneath somewhere, but I backed off out of that place and never did I try it again [*laughs*]. It's all closed in now, there was four *géag*s of the bush apart and one like a thumb straight up, it was a white thorn bush; they always said it was a hand – old superstitions all the time I suppose – of the woman who brought the bucket of holy water for the cow. I don't know now. There you have the history of that.

We reclaimed a part alongside the great wall and we raised different clay entirely from the rest of the land. It was a reddish clay, well it may not be a fact, but it looked like a skull we ploughed it up, that was 60 years ago, when it was talking about work they were, not archaeology or whatever you like to call it! The grass is growing there now. I don't bother touching anything. That well frightened me. But underneath that bush there was some kind of subterranean place, because the 6ft steel bar I had went all – whatever truth there is that it is a blessed well, I don't know. I won't go finding out.

PAULINE: *So you were born in Ballinaquive, and was there many in the family?*

There was seven – well there was eight? A local little girl died, in 1929, she died of diphtheria and my father – of course at that time everyone had to go to the wake – he went over to the wake. He was 39 years of age at the time and he came back from the wake and then a fortnight or three weeks later his daughter got it, Kathleen, and she died with it. She was eight. And about three weeks after it he died of it. He was only 39. There was 7 of us left then. The youngest was only four months and a half. And I remember that time there was no phonecalls to the hospital or anything. They phoned their local post office, and Jack Higgins, he was a worker there at the time, and he arrived outside the house and I was only a kid, I was only four years and a half, and I could see my mother crying and a next-door neighbour came in – he arrived on a horse and back, with a telegram, to tell us that he was dead. That was 1929. I grew up then.

I went to the old school in Labane, about 100 yards from the new school. It was a big room entirely, no partitions or anything. And there was two teachers, and there was a hut outside with another teacher who had the first and second-class children. Fr Considine, he was after coming a year or two before that into the parish from Gort, and he opened a graveyard alongside. We were as children sitting up on the walls looking in, running across to where the graveyard was. And the first lady, the first girl that was buried there, she was Conole, from Castletaylor. And that was about 1931, I think. The old school then was there, and John Flanagan retired, and a man by the name of Tommy O'Meara, he was a brother of the Tipperary hurler, Skinny O'Meara, he came to teach us. He was a new teacher, and the new school was built in 1934, I think, 'twas opened, and we went in there, and there was 111 children going to school that time. Three teachers. Alongside the new school then was the old hall, and Fr Considine went to build a new hall, which is there still. The old one was burned down and he took the stones from it and built this new master hall there, and he drew stones from Joe Murphy's yard, over beyond Moneen, Roxborough, and then he put up the grand gate. There was a grand gate he drew back and he put it up beside the church, and Martin Connolly, who was a godfather of mine, he was a mason that time, he that built it, and he was great at stone-building, he built those gates. They knocked the school then and cleared it, and now the new road runs there.

PAULINE: *Did you enjoy school?*

Well I don't like to be boastful, but I was good as what was in it! Because at that time there was a teacher's premium, and this was a western circuit, and Tommy O'Meara picked the two best out of the class – is it a bit boastful to say that I was one of them? [*laughs*]. Myself and Molly Bermingham. They called it the Carlyle and Brigg Premium, that was the name of it, to show the teachers' ability to teach. He won it, I got a hurl and Molly got – I don't know what she got. She was from Coxtown. I hope that wasn't boastful now!

I finished school when I was 14 years of age, and the first job I took on then was working with a neighbour. Well you were hired then, they called them the dog days, you'd be hired for a week, thinning turnips, mangolds, and all that, but I did keep one secret. They had a permanent workman that time, and he was getting 9 shillings a week, and the lady who was the boss of the house next door where I worked, I was getting 2 shillings a day, so I had to keep the secret from the permanent workman.

PAULINE: *And how were you getting so much?*

Well you see, they called them the dog days. I was only hired to do the dirty work, and I'd be laid off again, but he was permanent. All farmers had permanent workmen that time. 'Twas all slavery. But we were happy in our ignorance, if you like to call it. All had to be done by hand, the hay, the corn, the thrashing, you would go around with the threshing mill that time from one neighbour to another, handing bags, there was no bag less that two hundredweight that time, and some were up to twenty stone with wheat and that, it was all physical. Then, the station in Ardrahan, 1939, 1940, they put in the siding of the station, Gillane was the overseer that time, and we started a siding for beet, there were 45 wagons a day going out with beet to Tuam that time. It was a mainstay of south Galway and north Clare, beet. Over nights they brought them in, they were working till twelve o'clock. It gave money to all farmers who would do it, it was wonderful, but then we had a man who came along at a later day and said it wasn't making money, and closed it down. I was 45 years growing beet. It was work. First people used to thin it on their knees, then it got more advanced and they used to do it by hoes, and eventually they got a machine to pull it, and it was advancing all the time, but then they cut out the beet, they closed down Tuam, which was a scandal, shame. Ardrahan station then closed, and there was a co-op there, it was the oldest in Ireland, and all the fertiliser, manure, was all taken from there, everybody went down there, everything came by rail to Ardrahan for the locality. I remember as a young kid they brought down ten wagons of cattle at a time, a hundred cattle, from an uncle of John Bruton [*in Co. Meath*], and we drove them. I was in the driving of them into Kinvara, and there'd be men in Kinvara to take them to Carron. At that time you'd get 10 shillings for driving them, for the day, and ten shillings was some money that time.

PAULINE: *What about the fair in Ardrahan?*

Oh you want to hear that, do you? *[laughs]* Well, I was an able young man at the time, and he had a wild bullock, and he was an aged man. But there was fairs that time held in Ardrahan, there'd be a May fair, and an August fair, and markets around the 8th of

December. But he had this beast to go anyway, a year and a half, and I brought him down with him, and he said he'd give me £1 if I could keep him under control – which I did – and we held him out till the barrack in Ardrahan. And Martin Ayden, he was a buyer that time, he was one of the elite buyers, he was recognized as one of the best, and he bought the bullock. But – it was the 8th of December and there was Mass in Labane, and of course it was a mortal sin that time to miss Mass, and the bell rang in Labane, and I said, 'Whatever about the bullock, Pat, I must go to Mass'. 'O blast the hell', he said, 'what go to Mass and leave the bullock in the middle of the street to me'. 'Well I have no choice', I said. 'Lookit', he said, 'go down that place down there to the Protestant church', he said. 'They'll be all the one yet' [*laughs*].

PAULINE: *And I was asking you the last day, why do they call you Carty?*

Going to school we had Tommy O'Meara, he was a brother of the great Skinny O'Meara. Tommy O'Meara hurled with Galway in the late 1930s, but he was a great hurler. I had a team, there was school teams that time, and we went up to Gort to meet him, Kilbeacanty, and of course I was nearly as tall that time as I am now. I was going on 6 foot I suppose, and I was playing full back, but there was two lads that was nearest my size and I was pushing them out of the way, but I was the cause of winning the match, and Kilbeacanty objected afterwards that Ardrahan school had an outside player by the name of Carty. They thought I was Carty from Gort, Stephen Carty the publican. But they lost the objection then when they came to the school and saw me there with the rest! The crowd I was going to school with called me Carty afterwards.

We had twelve children, God bless them, and they're alive and well, the eldest boy now he is over 50. I got married below in the – what do you call it, the Iveagh Hotel – we got married in Labane, but that was where the reception was.

PAULINE: *Not many people used to go for receptions that time.*

Well, her uncle was a priest and that time you had to be fairly snobbish enough, hadn't you? [*laughs*] That's 55 years ago now. You'd never think 'twas that length. There was 5 boys and 7 girls. And they were all called after the names of the older generations.

Mick Dan Nolan was a little farmer, he was about 80 when I was growing up. He sang in every pub in Gort, and he was the first man I ever heard singing 'The Fields of Athenry' and the story was then told about the fields of Athenry by Kelly the poet, he was journeyman, he composed a lot of poems and songs, they say he composed 'The Fields of Athenry' which I heard 65 years ago. After the fairs the farmers went for a good few drinks, which I enjoyed even though I was young. Mick Dan Nolan would be short of money. He would cycle into town when the buzz was on in all the pubs, you would hear the boo with everyone talking and he would be asked to sing a song. People would buy him a pint and be delighted with his song, he sang everywhere that suited him. It is said that Jack Coppinger put the music to it, he was from Crannagh, he used cycle to Kinvara; the road from Ardrahan to Kinvara was across from Dunguaire castle, a fierce incline at that time and he went right in over the wall and was killed – that's a fact. Mick Dan Nolan had a great voice, he was a peculiar type of man, he never got up until evening, and he could dig spuds in the dark of the night.

About the fairs: myself and my brother would fill up the horse and cart, tea chests at the time, we would go to the market at St Patrick's Street we would leave home at 12 o'clock in the morning, 17 miles it would take 6 or 7 hours. In winter time get on the road with the horse the frost would be very bad that time, we would have to have horse nails in the horses' shoes. This night we went down to Galway we had to take hold of the horse and push it down the hill. In the wartime we would go to Limerick, 12 to 14 tea chests of apples. If you didn't sell them all there was a lock-in [*to store them*].

The fairs used to be held in different places, we had 3 fairs in Ardrahan, 3 in Kinvara, once a month in Loughrea and Gort, walk the cattle there in the middle of the night. If you had a bicycle and go out ahead of them you would be in clover. A young fellow needed to be out ahead of them because of gaps and boreens. You stood there all night, buyers from the north of Ireland, another man who used to export from the North Wall in Dublin, Cassidy was his name, all loaded in the station in Ardrahan and Gort, no lorries that time, all wagons. Rathkeale was the only factory in Ireland that time to go live on the hoof, an old bloke by the name of Hoarty went up to see 2 cows, to see them being killed in Rathkeale and when he came back people asked him what did they do with the bones and horns. Cows weren't skulled at all at that time. What did they do with them? He said nothing went astray only the dying screech.

We didn't know anything else only hard work. We would spend 5 or 6 weeks on our knees in the summertime.

That time there was only 3 cars in the parish; Lord Hemphill, the parish priest, and the Quinns had a hackney.

9 March 2004

Well, I was butler in Tulira Castle from the early 70s to the – into the 80s.

PAULINE: *Till it was sold, was it?*

No I was just gone before that, because as I think I mentioned it before to you, I was always on call, and I was married, and we had our own flat outside.

PAULINE: *Were you always on call?*

Yeah, you were on call you know, if anything came up, anything. Day and night, anything. And you know, when you're married, your wife expects you to be –

PAULINE: *home the odd night anyhow –*

Yes, I was always gone, eventually it was causing a bit of aggro, you know, and eventually I gave in my notice and we moved up outside Gort. My father was living on his own, and I got a job with the local County Council as a labourer. But during that time in Tulira, I did meet a lot of interesting people, and one of them was a former President of Ireland, President Childers, a nice man, and it was in Tulira Castle that President Childers met his wife, now I can't think of his wife's name [*Rita*] but that's where they met. They used to come there regularly enough, and they'd have their quiet dinner in the dining room, and then repair to the library for their brandy and ports, and there was a lot of interesting people, mainly a lot from the English gentry, the big estates in England, and in County Meath, and of course Charles Haughey used to call to Tulira regularly, more often than not with his wife; and former Taoiseach, Mr Cosgrave, Fine Gael, he called there, and then again there was a film made locally called *Alfred the Great*, directed by John Huston. John Huston spent a lot of time in Tulira, and I can't – John Ford, was it John Ford, I think so, yes into the film business too, and a friend of John Huston. And when that film was made, there was a lot of locals employed in it; they all had to grow beards.

And one man that impressed me deeply was the film star Paul Newman. Paul Newman stayed in Tulira on many occasions. On the first occasion Paul Newman was there for a weekend, and he bought a Connemara pony for his daughter, and actually 'twas I – he paid me in dollars for the pony, 'twas a thousand dollars that time, that was good money, big money, so I can say I had $1000 in my hand on one occasion! But I had to give it away naturally enough [laughs] unfortunately. So Paul – I think maybe you heard of Paul Newman and the Hole in the Wall gang – he started it up in Ireland where they look after children that are, well you know, special. Special place for them, take them on holidays and look after them. Actually Paul Newman and his wife are still married, which is unusual for a film star. But I did meet Paul Newman on a couple of occasions, very genuine, down-to-earth guy, and I met many ministers from the English government on different occasions. I met Mr Profumo, if anybody recognises that name!

Oh yeah I met a man by the name of Commander King, now he lived down there in Oranmore in a two-storey thatched house. He commanded two submarines in the last world war. He was married to the writer Anita Leslie and she was an ambulance driver at the front, rescuing soldiers; and Commander King at dinner parties in Tulira Castle generally would start about his experiences underwater with his submarine, and I remember I was serving, but I was still trying to listen, it was so interesting, that out of that English Channel, he was being shadowed by a German submarine, and it went on and on for hours, each of them giving each other the slip, but Commander King eventually got him and after that then he came home. He sank the German submarine, with an awful loss of lives naturally, and he was decorated for that, and he did command, I forget the name of the submarine, but he did command a second submarine later. But a great man to survive the war, but he could never settle on land, he always had the crave for the sea, the water, so he got a boat then, back in Galway then, a small enough sailing craft, and he set off to sail the world, and he did sail around the world, South Africa, all around, and he was a small enough man, thin and wiry.

PAULINE: *And would you be expecting these guests now, would you be told in advance who was coming you know?*

Oh yeah, yeah. We'd be told perhaps a week in advance. For the kitchen staff to have everything in order for the staff upstairs – including myself, everything in order, everything shining, silver, everything, dining-room floors, spick and span. I never spoke to anyone about who was coming and who wasn't. It was kind of a gentleman's agreement between Lady Hemphill and myself. She didn't say exactly to me, but it was expected, you just didn't carry stories, because you know, in dinner parties, life goes on and you just couldn't, I still wouldn't. Well I'd be watching [*laughs*]. But I never spoke about it to anyone and I never will.

PAULINE: *When you'd have a dinner party where would you stock up the house from, what would you have for dinners?*

Well the house was well-stocked always, a huge big larder that Lady Hemphill had, with all the spices and everything, stocked you know, a couple of big shoppings two times a year, in McCambridges in Galway, the meat was bought locally, the hens were bred for the eggs, they had a big garden that had everything.

But it was very interesting I must say, with the dinner parties coming up, and the dining-room table would be extended to seat, I think 'twas fourteen. There were candle-holders specially for those times, on the wall then were candles, no electricity in the dining-room – well there was, to keep the hotplates warm – but when the candles were lighting, all lighting, and the table was set and the silver gleaming and the special dinner things set out, and all the glasses for different drinks, and just to look at it, it was a work of art, really. That was my responsibility.

Then in the drawing room, having drinks before dinner, you could hear them all talking, and when we were ready to move, the cook and myself had to work together, and I'd open the drawing room door and announce, dinner is served. So I'd go back into the dining-room, stand there, Eileen Madigan, my helper, was at the other end of the table, and you'd be there standing behind the chair of the first lady that you were – and you could be there for one-half-hour, waiting. They'd be having their drinks. So again I might go in after fifteen minutes and announce, with a strong look at Lady Hemphill, dinner was served. And she'd say, 'Come on, come on, dinner's getting cold', and they'd all troop in and you'd hold a chair out for her, on the left-hand side of who was doing the carving, you'd hold a chair out for the lady who was to sit on his left-hand side, and you'd go around, and that was where the serving started.

It started there, and you went all around, and Lord Hemphill always carved, he did, he was good at carving, knew exactly where the seam was you know, and I'd be there by his side and we had a hotplate to keep it warm, but dinner was so big you know, you'd be going around a lot of times serving them all again, and then it could go on to half past eleven, midnight nearly. You'd be there, after serving then, you'd go out of the dining-room, and you'd go to the pantry. First of all you'd go into the drawing room, clean up the place, the drinks and everything else, re-set the glasses and stock up the drink tray, make sure they have enough for later on, and put out little snacks, a few logs on the fire, 'twas quite nice, you know, really and truly. After the first course then Lord Hemphill pressed the gong under his foot and it would start ringing in the kitchen and if you weren't on the ball, you'd hear it again. So you'd go in and you'd take each plate off each individual guest and you'd take them off to the pantry. And you'd come back in with warm plates for the second course, and so on, that's the way it went.

PAULINE: *And would you ever get frustrated now or would you ever –*

You'd be raging if the night wore on, you might have some appointment yourself, you might have a date with a girl, you might be going to a dance or a party yourself, you'd be raging. And I think when I was serving still some of the lady guests, wearing very low-cut dresses and I'd be coming in behind them serving the wine, having my eyeful and so on! But they were all extremely nice people, and if you made a mistake or anything, which I often did you know, a mistake in going to the wrong person at first, something like that, something stupid, it would be brought to my attention next morning.

Well the standard of living was extremely high there, and the standard of being looked after was extremely high. The guests that came there came into these big bedrooms with four poster beds, and their cases were unpacked for them, their nighties or whatever were left out for them, and you know they were extremely well-looked-after. And sooner or later they'd vacate the dining-room and go into the drawing room. And then we'd make a dash for the dining-room if there was going to be breakfast there next morning. Clear if off, get the table ready and put on a white tablecloth for breakfast. It was only used for breakfast the white tablecloth. In the morning then, you call each guest, tap gently on the door, and you went in with a tray of – silver tray with a cup of tea.

PAULINE: *And what time would you have finished the night before?*

Well it could be midnight, half-past-one, two. When they moved on into the drawing room, because once they vacated, that's all we wanted. Because generally they didn't bother us after that. And we'd go back down then when we'd made everything right upstairs. Back down to the staff quarters, sit down, Eileen had tea or coffee, I might have a half-drink of whiskey, then up to bed. And that was it.

PAULINE: *And what time did you start in the morning then?*

Started around 7, generally before it, because all the fireplaces had to be done, big roaring log fires, once the fire was on from early day, it was, with this high ceiling the hallway coming up, there was no doorway, it'd just be straight, sometimes you'd feel the whoosh, breeze coming up. Then each guest got their cup of tea in the morning, and came downstairs and into the dining room and had their scrambled eggs and rashers and cold meat and what have you, it was a big meal, breakfast, a really big meal, and then there might be a hunt on that particular day, the groom and the assisting staff in the stables would be getting the horses ready and the tack gleaming. Generally around half past ten or eleven o'clock they'd all take off in their hot-boxes, or the hunt might be in Tulira grounds, and they'd all meet in the courtyard, and you'd go around with port on a tray, and the girl, Eileen, would go around with sandwiches. They were very well looked after. Tulira was noted for its hospitality and James was noted for his freedom with the bottle! Because next morning, 'James, what did you do to me last night'. But Lord Hemphill was a generous man, in that line, you know. Very generous.

28 July 2003

PAULINE: *We're here now in Kileeneen. I'm talking to Mary Kate Connors, as I know her. Mary Kate, what's your maiden name?*

Kelly.

PAULINE: *And where were you born?*

In Cahirdine, Craughwell, over the last little inlet in the parish of Craughwell. It was three miles to school in Killeeneen and three miles home. Walk. In summertime take off the shoes. Miss Hanrahan taught us in our early two classes, then we transferred down to the Master, Mr. Kelly. Jim Kelly. There's grass growing over where we went to school. In the family were me and Jim and Nono. Nono died early this year. Our father and the next door neighbour's father – he was Mick Newell, the next door neighbour, and my father was Pat Kelly, and the two of them decided for their children to go to school they'd go to Kileeneen. There was too much traffic on the road to Craughwell. There was about three cars in the whole of the parish [*laughs*]. I left school at 14. I had great ambitions to go nursing, or to get educated. And the Lord knew best. My mother died when I was about to go somewhere, do something, and I stayed at home. Making bread, milking cows, feeding calves.

PAULINE: *You were running the house.*

Doing as best as I could.

PAULINE: *Was your sister younger than you?*

She was yeah, she finished in sixth or seventh class, she stayed at home as well. And Jim was working the land. With his father. So we all did our stint on the land. Hard work, picking potatoes, do you know, there was never a dull moment. Never a dull moment. Dadda died in 1958. Mother died 1939. I knew Mickeen since knee-height. He'd come to my grandmother's house, and I was always there, he was doing the work. I thought he was a nice lad, that's how it happened.

PAULINE: *Mickeen was lovely.*

He was, he was. He was a modern man of the days, like. He knew how to drive a car and he was a great cook and he was very sociable. We got married in 1966, and we lived here with Mary, my aunt. You remember Mary, so she was in great form when I arrived here. She was six years – I was six years here, before she died. And I nursed her for about fourteen months before she died. She was a good worker. So I looked after her then. She died 1972, aged 82. She was one of the Corbetts, my mother's sister. They were Corbetts from Kileeneen Beg.

PAULINE: *Did you know anything about Lady Gregory when you were a child?*

Well we didn't, 'twas more Antaine Raftery who was all the time being spoken about. And ah, she'd come into a conversation, but otherwise I knew nothing about the lady at all. And Raftery then was buried next door.

PAULINE: *What would you hear about him now?*

Where he spent his days on the south of Galway, he was in the Loughrea area, the Gort area, he travelled around, place to place. Then Craughwell was a great place of his, he used stay over in Callanans in Cahirdevane, and he stayed down in Cloonas, and that's where he died, in the year – I can't say the year now, he died Christmas Eve, and the fact that it being Christmas they didn't like to have remains in the house overnight, so they decided they'd bury Antaine Raftery, Christmas Eve, they got their – means of transport I suppose, horse and car, and came back the high road, by Cahirdevane here to Kileeneen. Cold night, and candlelight they were burying the remains, and Terry Furey, a young fellow at the time, held the candles while the work was going on. Even though the wind was so high and everything, the candles never quenched. That's what we were told anyhow. It's a tradition. Then he had friends, the Callanans of

Cahirdevane, if they were friends. They'd be friends with each other some times and they'd be at each others' throats some other occasions. Then they'd write derogatory poems about each other. They were always kind of messing with each other. Callanans thought they were more superior to Raftery. I wouldn't think they were, but [*laughs*].

PAULINE: *Had Raftery any relations around this area?*

No, no. Cill Aodáin. He just moved around. He was supposed to have a wife and a child, whether that was true or not I don't know.

PAULINE: *What's changed in Kileeneen since you came here?*

God bless the hare since I started going to school! Oh my God, thatched houses all over the way, Corbetts, Conlons, Feeneys, Keanes. Keanes had a slate house, although they had a thatched house, but they slated it about 1935, they took away the thatch. Who else had it, thatched house here, thatched house next door, Corbetts, thatched house Corbetts beyond, Callanan's thatched house, Ryder's thatched house, Forde's thatched house, Hynes had a two-storey house, slate house. 'Twas all thatch. All thatch.

PAULINE: *You'd know everybody?*

Oh you'd know the ins and outs of everybody. It was nicer. More friendly. And there were great characters here in the village. They'd have time for you. Great visiting place. Every night there was somebody walking in and out. Sundays they'd be visitors, the lads would be out there at the pump. There was an awful [*big*] generation of young people around the place, men especially, they'd be down at the pump every Sunday playing pitch and toss. Do you know the money, and you'd make a bob, and fetch the pennies. Whoever would be nearest to the bob would fetch the money, and it was a great game, they'd toss the coins then – it's a system in itself, I wouldn't know much about it, but I often saw them playing pitch and toss.

The road wasn't like it is now. The dust, dirt road that time was entertainment. They had their own hurling team. We often went to Gort, they'd hire a bus, we were only kids, to see Kileeneen playing. They had their own local team. So that was it. All agriculture. Beet and the potatoes and corn. All that had to be done. The weather was a big thing. Didn't every house have geese. The geese – when the goslings would be hardy enough, they'd transfer the geese, the old gander and the mother geese up to the turlough, after the Whit, after the first, because Whit always brought rain. And the geese would be all brung up to the river, and they'd be there all the summer then. And sometimes you'd go up and see your own crowdeen and I had them and I used call the gander Mailleogs, because there was a play one time, Mailleogs was its name, and I called the gander Mailleogs, and when I'm shouting Mailleogs you'd hear him, he'd answer back. He'd know your voice. You'd be so long there pampering them at home. They'd know you. It's like a dog'd know you.

The birds are clever too, I tell you. We'd leave them up there. I remember once I left them up there and it was an awful bad evening, and it rained so heavy that the turlough flooded overnight, and the geese moved away, and when I got up Sunday morning I was going to Mass in Craughwell, and when I got up to the gate, going to Mass, what was outside the gate only the gander, the geese. They came down themselves. Even though they had to come into the main Craughwell-Kileeneen road, they came as far as the boreen where I lived, and they came down. They had an instinct. But everyone had geese up there that time. And everyone had their sheep. And their cattle. And their horses. Cows – oh if you didn't watch the cows in the morning now, the cows want their drop of water in the morning in the river, you'd be drowned, they'd be gone across the river, they wouldn't come back

PAULINE: *It was a great system to have the turlough, wasn't it?*

'Twas, everyone paid a little rate then for their use, I'd pay half an acre, when your rate time came around. 'Twas commonage. Everyone could use it, but then there were some smart people bringing in outsiders, abusing the system. Oh the turloughs were great.

PAULINE: *Had you a story to tell me about when you were a young girl?*

A young girl [*surprised*]. Sure what did we do, we never went far, fair in Kileeneen, there were dances there, start around 9 and finish around 2 or 3 – if 'twas for a hurling night, they'd get two or three fellows with a banjo, local lads. Oh they used be coming from all directions for the dance there. Kileeneen Hall. Oh we thought it was a palace. We were every Sunday night beyond in it. It was, I suppose, two bob, and there might be a hop during the week, fourpence for the hop. And there was always a circus in the village, they'd have their tents and they'd be perched there near John Furey's. Gordy's was one crowd. And they used be over in the hall then. They'd have their sleeping accommodation outside and they'd have their acting and whatever inside. Oh they were good, very good. Gordy's.

PAULINE: *What kind of dancing would you be doing that time?*

It had to be half-sets. Half-sets and old time waltzes. Stack of Barley. They'd come from Labane parish, they'd come from Athenry, Tubber. All on bikes. They'd park their bikes in Callanans' shed, they'd park them in here.

I remember when your grandmother came from America, fifty years, I remember it well. I know I didn't want to go to school that morning, and my father said, 'Oh go on, get up, go to school, you'll see the Yankee when you're coming home then'. That made me stir. I went down to school and I saw Babe. I was her friend from the day I met her until the day she died. We were best friends. She was lovely, a lovely person. She had the gramophone coming back from foreign, and there was always half-sets around the big kitchen. Peggy Forde and I used to be there listening, taking in everything you could say.

PAULINE: *And she only came home for a holiday I think.*

Your great-granny used to be praying and praying that Babe would come back again. She used to go to Dublin then to renew her passport. Every three months, I don't know what was the period, the story'd go out that Babe was gone to Dublin to renew her passport, next thing she'll be going back again. And every time she went up she got me something, a necklace or something. And your granny'd be sitting this side of the fireplace and your granddad – your great-grandad, the other side. And all of them would come to visit. She met Johnny then at a dance in Craughwell – I think it was Michael Fahy that introduced them, and that's how the romance started. And she never went back. And the day she got married then, we were at school, and we were brought in on our way back from school. 'Twas a lovely wedding. Must be around springtime, but she was a lovely lady. That's where ye got all yeer looks from.

PAULINE: *Tell me a bit more about the dances.*

The dances! 'Twas all right for those that had their mothers at home, they'd get great lectures before they'd go out that time. The likes of me, I had no-one to say hello or how to avoid the dangers, so, learn how to dance and you'd get popular then.

PAULINE: *Was it hard to get the two shillings?*

Oh nothing in the world was as hard! To get the two bob. You'd be asking it and begging it and doing jobs for someone that'd be *flaithiúl*. It was a lot, 'twould nearly buy all the groceries for you for the week. 'Twould go a good way.

PAULINE: *And how often would you expect to get out?*

Every Sunday evening. Every Sunday evening. You'd have to. Sure God wouldn't you die with the ... There used be a mineral bar too –

PAULINE: *And used the priest be in there?*

Oh God no, he would not.

PAULINE: *I thought the priest used go down to the dances that time?*

Oh he didn't approve of them, he'd be shouting off the altar – now before my time – Fr Tully he was down on dances, he called it a hell of a hall he called it. And sure that was the only means of people meeting. Next thing they built the hall in Craughwell. And this place here was forgotten about. Posh place over in Craughwell. And they all left here. 'Twas about 1949 I'd say. And then the big bands were coming in. There was one great night always, the sheep-breeders night, the 22nd of January, the Sheepbreeders, you know people who had sheep farms, they'd come down from Tipperary, and from – it was a great occasion. And 'twas always raining or snowing or something. Watch out for the Sheepbreeders' dance they'd say because the climate would come very, very bad that period of time. Oh 'twould be a great night, you wouldn't be able to move. 'Twould be choc-a-bloc.

15 February 2004

I was born in a place called Annaghdown parish townland not far from Headford. I was born in 1920, that's a while back. I went to school in Corrandulla National school there and – I never told a story like this now, you know more about that now than what I do, so you'd better ask questions and I'll be answering the questions.

PAULINE: *You told me you were a great dancer?*

I was. I started dancing when I was 10 years.

PAULINE: *And what gave you the interest?*

Well there was a few dances about the place and I liked the dancing, the parents liked the dancing, and they got me into it. I got the lessons in my own house from a man from Galway who played the fiddle, he used to come out to the house once a week. Well, they were very friendly with my family, and he was taught in Cork, the man that taught me. So we had a grand time. In a most amazing amount of time I learned the dancing, jigs, reels, the hornpipe, Blackbird, Job of Journeywork, everything. And I would go to the feises, I was going to the feises when the feises used be out in the field. I went to feises every place there was one, there was one many place that time, around the place. There used to be a feis in my own parish, and I used to go to down to Clare, in every town there was a feis. All over the place. There was no dressing up. I used to dance in the Connacht championship now, and my dress-up was a black pants and a white shirt, there wasn't dancing shoes, there was no dancing shoes that time, just the ordinary pointed toe shoe.

PAULINE: *And what did your friends think of you doing this now?*

Ah, they were delighted sure, they'd be delighted when I'd win a prize and come home celebrating. The nearest feis I danced here was Kilbeacanty. I danced till I was – well, I'll tell you, I was 53 years when I danced.

PAULINE: *From since you were 10 maybe?*

Yes. I danced up in Claregalway. Cycled it. There was nothing else, only the bike –

PAULINE: *You could cycle twenty miles?*

I did, and more than twenty miles! And go to a dance after coming home! We enjoyed life, and it was a grand life, and it was a peaceful life and it was an enjoyable life.

PAULINE: *And what has changed, do you think, with people?*

Ah sure you wouldn't know what has changed with the people – I'll tell you, too much money, they have too much money now. Much better quality of life that time, we made our own sport, and we were enjoying ourself at the same time. And there was no drinking, I wasn't drinking at all.

PAULINE: *Used you go into Galway much?*

Oh sure we were in Galway ever. That time, I used to bring hay in a horse and cart into Galway from where I lived, and sell it. 'Twas a great life for young people that time.

PAULINE: *Do you still follow it [the dancing]?*

Oh I do surely. And do you know what I tell you? When I hear Irish dance music I cry, I cry with sadness. I'd love to go dancing. But it was a lovely pastime for any young boy or girl, and do you know, there wasn't many girls at all dancing that time, all boys. Quite the opposite now.

PAULINE: *Were there many in your family?*

Ten children in my family, and there were three dancers in it. I'm the last one of my generation alive.

PAULINE: *Where did you meet your wife?*

At Seapoint! That's where I met her. And she was a nice girl, from Co. Laois. She was working. Working in

Seapoint, so I used to get free tickets [*Laughs*]. I used. I got married in 1952.

PAULINE: *You weren't too young.*

I wasn't. But there was no-one getting married young that time. We went to Dublin on honeymoon, it was the first time we were ever in Dublin, we stayed in – Hayden's hotel I think. Ah sure, 'twas a long way to get – I got up at six o'clock in the morning to go down to get married down in Laois, and I had a fellow from – I had a car from Galway. And do you know what he charged me to go down to Laois for the one day – ten quid. 'Twould get you nowhere now.

PAULINE: *How did you go to Dublin then?*

On the train. We had a good old time. And you'd make a lot of friends with dancing. You'd meet their parents, and they were lovely dancers too, the old people.

PAULINE: *What kind of work did you do when you left school?*

I was working around at home, the land, not killed working but I did work hard, I did work hard. So he gave me the farm then, and I settled down, I was the third son. The other lads went to England. They did, they wouldn't stay at home, they didn't like farming. So he left me the farm. And our land, where I was born that time, was very fragmented, pieces here and pieces there, so, I said to my father one time, I think we'll change out of this and buy a farm together. Oh no, he said, you'll not get a right place if you sell that. So that settled that. But didn't my son do it! But he didn't do what I told him. I advised him to do it. I was delighted he did it. He bought a place different altogether. We moved here sixteen years ago. I was lucky, the people I met. They are wonderful people. I love it here. Years ago I wanted to move but my father didn't want to and I didn't want to go against my father, you know, didn't want to break his heart. But I was happy to get the change. But there were three neighbours now here in Ardrahan and I could never forget them. Tom Fahy, Tom Moylan and Ger Fahy. When we came up here my son's wife got laid up, she had to go down to Cork to have an operation on the brain, and we had cows, and they wouldn't let me out. They'd come to the door at night and tell me not to go to the cows, they'd look at them in the morning.

I never did any cardplaying in my life. I was always dancing. Dancing, dancing, dancing, and that was all I wanted to do.

9 February 2004

I was born 6th of May 1913. A good while ago! [*Laughs*].

PAULINE: *And was there many in your family?*

Nine. I went to National school in Labane.

PAULINE: *And did you like school?*

I hated it! [*Laughs*].

PAULINE: *And what age did you leave then?*

Fourteen. You had to go till 14. Then I went gardening in Tulira. First I went into Whiriskeys in Ardrahan. It was farm work mostly. They had a fair good farm. They hadn't a big lot of land any of them but they had a fair amount, and there was one of the farms a stand for the corn for the winter, three or four stones, put them standing roundabout and put the corn up on it, you put maybe ten layers of wheat thrown there, that'd be lovely in the winter then, the man would come in and thrash it, 'twould be fresh and clean and grand. And – I suppose you often had porridge? There was oatens too, we put oats too, in the open, 'twould be clean, no dirt, the Taylors used clean it anyway. They had a big mill in Athenry and they used to work, they sold there when they got tired of farming, the Land Commission bought it. There was two of them there, they had 100 acres each. Ben and Dick. John Henry was in the hotel. After that I went to Tulira and I worked in the garden, for Hemphill. So I suppose I'm 20 years retired, am I?

PAULINE: *Where did you go dancing when you were young? Where was there a dancehall?*

There wasn't a touch of a dancehall that time, we were at an old barn dance, 'twould be a dance in a barn, so much to eat, there'd be tea going and everything.

PAULINE: *And where was your parents' family home then, was it here?*

My father met my mother when she came working to Tulira. My father was a butler in Tulira, and mother was a Kilkenny woman. My father was from Tullamore. We got this farm then from the Land Commission. We were entitled to land then. We walked into it. House built and all. They worked for Martyns. Mr Martyn was the owner of the land. I met Edward Martyn. He'd go to Mass in Labane and they'd wheel him down the road. My father was a butler in it and he'd wheel him down.

7 December 2003

PAULINE: *Today is Sunday, the 7th of December 2003. Did you know the Black and Tans?*

I remember when they came into the house, in Coxstown, and my father said to my mother 'You go down ...' he said, 'because', he said, 'if they saw a man they might shoot him'. They'd shoot you, you know, and Mom went out, and sure she said, 'We don't know anything about the Black and Tans' because somebody was shot in Castledaly, and they thought we knew, and my poor father – God be with him now, he'd go in and do a dance for you – and he said he didn't know anything about the Black and Tans, and he was ploughing down the field, he heard it, that there was a man shot in Castledaly, and sure we don't know who shot the man in Castledaly, and they come to my father. He had a gun for them, pigeons and that, so, anyway, we got over all that. But we used to be very frightened of them coming. And they come in one day, and I had a lovely sister, Agnes, she was very beautiful, and when they came in, they told us to get out of the house, and Agnes said, 'I'll get out when I get my prayerbook and when I'm ready'. And as she walked into the front room, if she didn't have turned as she did, down to the right to get her prayerbook, she'd have been shot dead. He fired the bullet, and we had the bullet a long time in the house, and he fired at her for saying that. Some brat of a fellow, I suppose, I mean he wouldn't be trained to do that, I don't think so, no.

My mother used to be – God help her, she was only small, I'm like her, I'm the only one like her, she was one of the Kellys from Rockmorris, Tubber. I was like her. There was bullets flying all around the road outside, and they'd fire bullets up at the chimney top. That chimney top was only done a few years you know, they put holes in the chimney top, but I think they were drunk, they were very drunk that time, you didn't know who they were. And I remember I saying to Mattie my oldest brother, Lord have mercy on you Mattie, I remember him saying, he was older than me, and I caught him by the hand and I said, 'We'll go on, we'll go way down the fields' and we had nothing, we had no shoes, no stockings, no nothing, I had a shift on me that I went to bed on, and we went down to the end of the land, the end of Forde's house, the house is still there, Annie Forde, and we hid there nearly all the night.

I was shivering with the cold, we came back, we heard them shouting, they were screaming and shouting outside Howleys, and we came back, then, oh, that night, my poor mother, and they said, 'What age is the oldest boy?' They were going to shoot him, and that was Mattie, but Mattie escaped with us. We went away down the fields and we were there all night. It's a wonder we're alive, honest to God, people don't know what we went through, and came up in the evening [*sic*], when all was quiet, we had to go to school –

PAULINE: *Was that 1920, 1921?*

I don't know what year, I didn't sorta bother about years, but we, ah, the teacher Mr Doyle stayed in our house during the war you see. I was there, ara sure he never drank, he'd nip up with my father, down to Bradleys, have one or two. I think he liked it, but he was a nice man, and Eileen my sister was lovely, she's in America, she's still alive, she was the only one of us with a brain, and the teacher wanted her to go to be a teacher, but my father hadn't got the money, that time you had to pay, see, he hadn't got the money, and she was lovely Eileen. She married a Dutchman, but he died, but the children keep in touch with me, they're lovely children. She wanted to come back to Ireland, she came back once to see Pop and Mom, she didn't come too often. She was lovely, she was very nice to me, and she married that man. He was a nice man, an artist really, he could paint, do anything with his hands, he was a lovely man, he was crazy about her, and I think he died before her.

PAULINE: *Jerry told me to ask you about the floods.*

Here? Sure the floods were – as you go up to Peterswell, we were nearly drowned there, we went out in an old boat that was only patched together, gee, wasn't I awful. I was a wild devil you know, and we went out there, and I thought we'd never get back. 'Can you swim?' says one of them. 'No, I can't swim' but I could swim a bit, but I said, 'I'd be frightened to swim there, this isn't a place for swimming, you'd get drowned'.

PAULINE: *If you were going to write a book what would you write about? Would you write about your childhood?*

I'd start at the beginning when I left Ireland, that's what I would do, that's what I think. When I left Ireland the first time I went to New York. And I went out to Uncle Tom, my father's brother. He was a lovely man and he had two daughters and two sons. I loved New York, really liked it. But I liked England better than anywhere. Whatever they say about the English, they're nice people. They're really gentry, and nice, and when I met the English, they couldn't believe I was Irish you see, and I said, 'yes I'm Irish'. So I met this lady and she said, 'would you like to work for me'.

Well 'I'm looking for something for the time being, I don't know what I'll do'. I did cashier business, I was good at the numbers, so I worked with her, and the children, the children were lovely, and I used to dress the little one up, like a doll, but they were sort of – Jews, like. Their religion was different to mine, but they never minded me blessing myself and talking to them about God – you know, I was there a good while, they liked me very much, they didn't want to part with me, but I said, 'goodbye'. I said I'd be back again, but I never did. I met Michael there, my husband, and he was in Blackrock College, he was going to be a priest or something, well he had ideas about it, and then he changed his mind when he met me.

PAULINE: *You changed his mind for him!* [*laughs*]

I did. I changed his mind. We got married later. My mother and father were crazy about him. I brought him home before we were married, and I said, 'they might throw you out now when they see you' – my mother liked him and my father liked him.

PAULINE: *Music was very important in your house at home was it?*

Music. We all loved it in Coxtown. You should hear it of an evening. We went into the front room, and the fireplace was there, we had a fire. Pop and Mom was sitting outside in the kitchen, in the other room. Well you should hear Joe playing. He'd bring in the fiddle, and they'd have a flute. I used to play a flute – we used to have a great band, and Mom used to roar laughing at him, we used to do that regular. 'Twas lovely. We were noted for music, like, see, I would say 'Pop what are you putting the boots on for' he used to say, 'mind your own business', put the boots on, well you see we had no carpet on the kitchen floor, that's why he put the boots on, you should hear the noise he made! Oh he was a marvellous tap-dancer you know, my father.

Chris said to me one day not too long before she died, she said, 'Baby', she said, 'do you know but I had a lovely father'. I know, he never told us off, and Mom would say, 'be back here at ten o'clock tonight, wherever you're going'. 'We will Mom, but leave the window open won't you'. She'd leave the side window open. 'And don't make any noise' [*laughs*].

PAULINE: *And where would you have been? Where were you gone?*

Well we just went around to the neighbours talking and dancing, maybe down to Labane, we'd be late coming back –

PAULINE: *What was in Labane?*

Well there was music, there was always music in Labane, there was. We were very friendly with the Quinns, you know Quinns' shop. Mrs Quinn and my mother were like that, but Maura Quinn, Maura died, 'tis terrible how things change, they died and they got old and one thing and another,

PAULINE: *What year were you born?*

Don't be asking me! I'm not going to tell you. I'm awful old. What age would you say I am?

PAULINE: *Are you eighty?*

Eighty-four. I had blonde hair when I went to America. My mother was very beautiful when she was young and I'm the only one like her.

PAULINE: *Were there many in your family?*

Well, Agnes was lovely, she died at 27, she was beautiful, she was a diabetic, but that time they didn't know anything about it. She'd be alive today, they found about all the sugar, and she was on insulin, injection, she was on that for years. She had big brown eyes and jet black hair, on my father's side, and she is buried in Peterswell.

PAULINE: *And was your mother musical?*

She was, she could sing lovely, every time we went out, 'Baby' they called me, 'Baby, your mother will sing a song'.

PAULINE: *What would she sing?*

Ah sure, old-fashioned, 'After the Ball was over' that kind, you know, and 'Two Little Girls in Blue' things like that, she didn't know anything else like. She did know a few things, she was very smart like … She loved the boys. Four boys she had and seven girls.

PAULINE: *Were you the youngest?*

No. they just called me Baby. They said I looked like a baby, and my mother said to me, 'you're the best-looking of the lot of them', she said, 'because you have lovely blonde hair'. It wasn't blonde, it was more ash-colour, I had lovely yellowy hair, and long, and when I went to America, I could sit on it, they cut it in America, a bit of it, they didn't cut it all, but it managed to grow again. When I went to England they said, oh cut your hair, you're much nicer with it cut, so they cut the hair for me in England, so I let it grow again.

PAULINE: *How long did it take on the boat to America?*

I think we were eleven days on the water, but I was so sick I'm telling you straight I prayed to die, I vomited. When I got there then Uncle Tom was there to meet me, sure I suppose I looked like a corpse, I looked terrible, but I'm not used to it, but I had nice cousins there. I didn't see much of them, they were all working, and they were tired in the evening and one thing and another –

PAULINE: *What were you working at over there?*

Well I, I worked for a guy called SR Hogan, I never forgot his name, he was always looking at the girls' legs. I loved this girl, she come from County Cork, what was her name, she'd go out you know and she'd do this, the way she'd know he was looking, she was grand, poor Hannah. I don't know where she is, maybe she died, you see we didn't keep in touch too much, there was too many of us, and Bridie come from, she was old-fashioned, she came from Clare, was it, no Mayo. I don't know where she is, Bridie was nice. Jessie came from Scotland, she was a scream that one.

PAULINE: *What kind of work were you doing?*

Well the only work, if you worked in a house, you dusted everything every day, we had an awful easy life in America that time. But I didn't work all that time. I was with Uncle Tom for a while, and I went to New Jersey. We had a holiday out there, because they had a home there, wealthy, they came to see me one time, then one day I said to him, 'Uncle Tom, I'm awful homesick, I have to go home to see my Mom and Pop'.

PAULINE: *How did you come home?*

Boat again, it was cheaper, and there was no flying much that time. God almighty they were glad to see me. I said, 'the food is lovely in Ireland and I'm not going back' and I went to Dublin, there was a cousin of mine in Dublin. She said, 'Baby if you come out to me you can stay here'. 'Oh all right', I said, 'I am going to England', I said, 'but I'll stay', and she'd met Michael. I think Michael had stayed there for a couple of days, she liked Michael, and she said, 'Michael is here'. 'Oh is he?' I quite liked her you know, now, but I couldn't live with her, so anyway I arrived and met Michael, and we sort of kept in touch, and I said I'd be going away – where – I was going to Birmingham, so I said 'I'll write to you', and he said, 'All right'. And then when I wrote another time he said he was coming to see me and he came to see me and I thought, well I like him. He was from Drogheda, I loved Michael.

Kathleen was delighted, Nora was delighted, they were all delighted that I met him, and he stayed, so we thought then we'd get married and have a place of our own. It would be better, cheaper and everything, and that's what we did, and I always lived a good life. We didn't – you know.

So anyway he stayed, he was lovely, and he was never sick or anything, and we weren't long together when he died, and why God took him I don't know. He wasn't sick, pain in his chest or something, and he didn't drink a lot, he took a drink to be sociable, he smoked a bit, but not too much I think, that was Michael. He was nice-looking, jet black, black hair, lovely face, lovely skin.

Myra 2nd from left
30 September 2003

Myra is living in Rathbaun. She was from Newquay in County Clare. Myra Keane was her maiden name.

Newquay was a great seaside resort, the school was right beside our house, the school had no playground. They used our field. It was a two-teacher school with about 50 students. Two of my sisters went to England, I stayed at home. I got the whooping cough at twelve, nearly died, I was anointed. It was rather late when I finished school. I got pleurisy afterward, I was a bit weak so I stayed at home.

Myra wanted to tell me about an experience she had when going to school.

I was only about seven or eight and the teacher was sending me to the shop for change, Nilands shop. This very rough day it was in winter time, the townland where the school was, Ballyvaughan, the town at the mouth of the lakes, there are two lakes in it. A very stormy day in winter there was a flood in the road and at that time there was no wall on the lake to prevent the water. When I was coming out I was blown out into the lake. I had the note in my hand, it was a ten-shilling-note to change. There was a man going over the road with a bucket of water from the well. I shouted at him, he was deaf and didn't hear me there. I was in the lake with the water up to my neck. I caught a big stone and I managed to survive and came up to the road again, went into school and on home to change my clothes. I was more worried about the note I had in my hand than myself. I never forgot that day. I got such a fright. They have a wall now in it.

My grandmother was Niland from Ardrahan, so I used to come on holidays. I was often over, my godmother introduced me to Peter Forde. He turned out alright, we got married in a short time. Older people were more plentiful. It was hard enough to please me. I had an intention of going into the convent. I knew a lot of people in Ardrahan, I had more friends around here than at home.

A silent thought, a quiet prayer;
For a special person in God's care.

In Loving Memory of
Mary Gardiner
Cregclare, Ardrahan, Co. Galway
who died on the 22nd of May, 2006.
Age 82 years.
R.I.P.

30 September 2003

PAULINE: *You are not from Ardrahan?*
No, I'm from Ballymana, Craughwell.
PAULINE: *What was your maiden name?*
Furey, Mary Furey.
PAULINE: *Was there many in your family?*
Ten.

PAULINE: *Ten children? Were there many boys?*

Six boys and four girls.

PAULINE: *You went to Ballymana National School?*

That's right.

PAULINE: *You all went there?*

Yes.

PAULINE: *Any further education?*

No.

PAULINE: *Nobody did that time?*

An odd lucky one.

PAULINE: *An odd one, here and there. What age did you finish school?*

Fifteen.

PAULINE: *What did you do when you finished school?*

Worked in shops and pubs.

PAULINE: *You had a few jobs then.*

And then I came to Ardrahan, to Taylors. I was in Taylors before I came over here.

PAULINE: *Who did you work for? Ellis?*

No, for his uncle John Henry Taylor.

PAULINE: *In the pub or hotel?*

The hotel, it was called a hotel years back.

PAULINE: *Had you many guests coming to it? Or what kind of hotel was it?*

No, not in my time. But before then. It was just a pub in my time.

PAULINE: *This is where McHugh's is now.*

Where they were. Yes.

PAULINE: *So you worked in a hotel there?*

I worked there for five or six years.

PAULINE: *So that's where you met your husband was it? Is that where you saw him?*

Yes. That's my history now.

PAULINE: *And you came here then.*

Yes, here I am.

PAULINE: *Where was he from originally?*

From Rathbane, one of the Gardiners. A brother of Miko's, and Eamonn was another one of them up in the Castle. The rest are all dead – Gerry, Frank and Paddy.

PAULINE: *So you worked in Taylors Hotel for John Henry Taylor, Was he married?*

Oh he was, he was an old man when I worked for him.

PAULINE: *Was he a Protestant? Some of them were Catholic.*

He was a Protestant.

PAULINE: *Was there many in his family? Had he children?*

Two girls.

PAULINE: *What were their names?*

Maureen and Eileen.

PAULINE: *I never heard of them.*

This is going back a long time ago.

PAULINE: *That would be Dick's and Ellis's uncle.*

He would have been.

PAULINE: *Who did he sell the place to then? Did McHughs buy it after that?*

Yes, it was McHughs after that.

PAULINE: *What kind of duties did you do in the pub?*

Selling drinks.

PAULINE: *Did they have a shop?*

No shop, just the pub.

PAULINE: *Life was different in Ardrahan in those times.*

Yes, very different.

PAULINE: *There were fairs in Ardrahan?*

Right you are. Out in the street yes.

PAULINE: *All into the pub afterwards.*

They would yes. They had all their pens up. Timber pens all over the village where they put their stock into them.

PAULINE: *Sheep and cattle.*

Sheep or cattle whatever would be on. When you think back, it's gone very modern since them times.

PAULINE: *That would be a good drinking day then.*

They would be in and out all day then.

PAULINE: *Would food be served?*

No food, just the drink.

PAULINE: *Porter?*

Pints usually, out of a barrel. They would tap a barrel them times. They'd turn a tap on a barrel.

PAULINE: *Did you live in?*

Yes.

PAULINE: *In a little flat?*

No, I lived in the house with the couple themselves.

PAULINE: *That is a nice interesting bit of news I hadn't heard before.*

I suppose it is, if you want to go back along the way.

PAULINE: *I'm trying to build up a picture of Ardrahan.*

Your father, God be with him, used to come in. He was only a young fellow at that time, maybe ten or twelve.

PAULINE: *He wasn't drinking, was he?*

Not at all, he came in for whatever his mother would send him for. He wasn't living in the house you are in now, he was living up at the end of the road there behind Whiriskeys, I think they lived there.

PAULINE: *Who was living in Ardrahan that time? Who had Taylors' shop? Was it Ellis?*

It was Ellis, and Dick was across in the big house.

PAULINE: *Moylans and Croppy Joyce?*

Yes and the Tarpeys, Kellys and Whiriskeys –

PAULINE: *Then Daddy's mother was in the corner.*

She was. Kate, a grand little woman she was.

PAULINE: *She only had one child.*

She just had him, her one and only.

PAULINE: *They moved over to Kinvara road.*

That's right and she loved you all as you came along. I used to hear them talking about her that she used to think that you were all – do you remember her?

PAULINE: *I do, I was nine when she died. There were eight girls born when she died.*

Imagine that, a treat for her as she had no girl.

PAULINE: *I don't know, was it, and then Peter arrived after she died.*

Have you another boy?

PAULINE: *Yes, Sean, and Roisin is the youngest.*

A big crowd all gone away, scattered everyplace.

PAULINE: *There are three living at home still.*

That's nice.

PAULINE: *Nobody went too far.*

That nice too, besides going away.

PAULINE: *Have you relations at home still in Ballymana?*

No, my brother died, there isn't anyone there now. I had two brothers who went to Australia. One in Australia died, I have one in England. Colman died in Australia a few years ago.

PAULINE: *When did they go to Australia?*

Oh they went in the 50s.

PAULINE: *It was very difficult to come home and travel that time. It is different nowadays, they can come and go.*

Everything was harder them times.

PAULINE: *Do you think life was harder?*

Oh yes, less money around. You had to do everything the hard way.

PAULINE: *Do you think times have changed?*

A lot of improvements.

PAULINE: *Financially anyway.*

Well yes around the house you have electricity. There was no electricity when I came here first or no running water, so that's a big improvement. You can't do without them now.

PAULINE: *If the electricity goes we are all panicking.*

That's right all panicking.

PAULINE: *Do you get much visitors now? In the evenings do people come in visiting you?*

Now? No, not really. I think visiting is gone out.

PAULINE: *Why do you think that is? What do you blame for that?*

Television I suppose, people sit down at home for their own entertainment. There was none in my time at home when we were young, people came in and out to visit which was nice.

PAULINE: *They didn't feel they were interrupting anything.*

No, it was the done thing.

PAULINE: *That is the one thing people say to me, the visiting is gone.*

I think it's sad, people will only come if they are invited.

PAULINE: *People don't want to come in, they don't feel free coming in.*

They don't do it because it's not done.

PAULINE: *It's gone and it won't come back either.*

It will never come back. Not with the young crowd now, if they go anywhere now it's to the pub for entertainment.

PAULINE: *Women didn't go into the pub when you worked there?*

Oh God no, if you were sent for to go into the pub for something you'd be embarrassed to be seen going in. What a change!

PAULINE: *More women in pubs now than lads.*

Yes and no remarks at all. There would have been no such thing as a woman having a drink except a mineral, maybe, in a group.

PAULINE: *What hours were in the bar that time?*

From nine in the morning to ten or eleven at night.

PAULINE: *Would people be drunk that time?*

They wouldn't be there all day. Passers-by and towards night then the few local people, they didn't have money like that to get drunk at night, just a few drinks and a chat. They liked coming in to visit.

PAULINE: *Would they play cards?*

No.

PAULINE: *Any music or anything?*

No, no such thing.

PAULINE: *Did people play music themselves?*

No, unless you'd get a fellow to sing a song.

PAULINE: *That was nice too.*

Very nice. It was nice. I liked it there. It was nice and peaceful. There was nobody to bother me. I was quite happy there.

PAULINE: *How did you get that job? Was it advertised? Or was it by word of mouth?*

A neighbour knew about it and told me. The lady who worked there got married. She lives in Gort still.

PAULINE: *What is her name?*

Mrs Donoghue.

PAULINE: *She worked there before you?*

She did.

PAULINE: *Thanks very much, Mary, that was lovely, that is news I never heard before.*

Do you know the Fahys up there? Their mother she was Irwin from back Ballyvaughan side I think. She worked there before Mrs Donoghue. She married up in Labane.

PAULINE: *People didn't work that time when they got married?*

Oh no such thing. They stopped then, that was it, they never worked again. Or they worked hard for no money. Work without pay.

PAULINE: *Which Mrs Fahy was that?*

She has a son there all the time. I don't think he is married. She has two daughters, they used to come home while she was alive, she died a few years ago. Mary and Ann.

PAULINE: *Did anyone else work in the bar or were you working on your own?*

They worked themselves early in the day and I cooked the dinner for them and they went in and I went out.

PAULINE: *What were the wages likes?*

Terrible, pence, no wages at all, very little.

PAULINE: *You had your keep?*

The money was bad.

PAULINE: *It was probably better than what other people were doing at the time. At least you were working.*

Yes. There were no jobs going much. Especially if you hadn't education. If you had you could go on, go nursing and different things. Lots of chances now for young people.

PAULINE: *It's great now.*

Well it is. It has improved now.

PAULINE: *It has improved and disimproved in other ways.*

Some of the good things have gone, some of the bad things are gone too.

PAULINE: *That's true.*

So that's the story. Will you have a cup of tea?

Colie on right

Born in 1919 in Ruanmore, he was the youngest of 12, came from an average sized farm. They produced all their own, killed a pig or a sheep, had no fridge, no electricity, no car, no wireless. They all went to Kiltiernan National School, there was no secondary school in south Galway.

Only looking forward to be 14, then stay at home and work here and there, earn a shilling. We all went to National School and all stayed at home at 14, some started to move out and went to England, some worked locally. It was hard to get the money to go to England that time. We went gradually, one after another. An American wake, it was the same thing going to England that time.

When I got to 20 years of age – that was 1939 – the war broke out and I joined the army. I stayed for the duration of the Emergency, 6 years. We were based in Athlone, Mullingar and Longford, Galway and a while in Dublin. We used spend a lot of the summer down in Finner camp in Donegal between Ballyshannon and Bundoran. I got into hurling with the Fourth Brigade, and with the Fourth Brigade we won the All-Ireland hurling championship in 1943–44, combined teams from Athlone and Mullingar barracks. The All-Ireland manoeuvres came up in 1943. We walked from Finner up along through Meath, Westmeath and Cavan and we landed in Westmeath for the championship. It was late and the stores were locked, only half of us had boots, we played a team called Castlepollard. The next day was Monday we headed off for the manoeuvres – the army was divided into two divisions A-B and we left Mullingar and walked for Clara, we camped for the night somewhere. One Sunday we walked from Thurles to Tipperary, 31 miles, it was the longest walk, average 3 half miles per hour. During the All-Ireland manoeuvres we had to cross the Blackwater in Fermoy, a big current there, we had to cross in full gear, two were drowned the same night.

It was harvest time, the corn was cut that time, there was no combines, all cut by hand, in stacks; someone dropped a match, the whole garden was ablaze, the farmer was probably compensated by the Government.

We crossed the Nore into the border of Kilkenny, we landed in the Curragh, we stayed the night, then off to the Phoenix Park for two weeks holiday after the manoeuvre. We stopped in a place called Clondalkin, the Paper Mills. I remember Dev, Frank Aiken and Sean Lemass came out to meet us, we were having a cup of tea – you can call it tea if you like! Dev came along and

he was sampling the tea, he took the tin mug and it w[...]
battered and he sampled it, so I can always say I had
'High Tea' with Dev. So we hit for the Park we stayed
there for two weeks we stayed in a tent – 'a holiday'.
We came back by train to Athlone.

10 November 2003

I was born, Pauline, in a very – put it this way I was born in the middle of the landlords, the de Burgos, the Burkes, were the principal ones, that's now that's related to the Queen of England, what was the name, the local name, Ballydougan, they're still there, one of the few families that'd be there three or four hundred years. They're the St John Burkes now –

PAULINE: *Where were you born, what part?*

I was born in a place outside Loughrea, Pauline, in a place they call the Racecourse. Now there's a racecourse outside Loughrea, I was born close to it, it's one of the oldest racecourses in Ireland. It ran – the first race it ran was possibly the end of the eighteenth century, because all around them you had the big landlords, you had the de Burgos, you had down the road, you had the Eyres of Eyrecourt, and you actually – and Albie de Burgo was of course representative of the English government in Ireland, so they started the racing sometime in the end of the 18th, and it went on till, a big race this was, it went on for three weeks. This is the part now I get mad about, because you see my father, and grandfather, and great-grandfather, they used to look after the racecourse between racing, and now my father had a little row of sheds, they were gone now by the time I was 15 or 16, and you see you must remember that time you had no trains or lorries to bring horses, horses had to come by road, so they'd be coming the week before the races, usually when the races were at their prime, the races went on for nearly three weeks, they would be three weeks now for my father and his grandfather, the ordinary racecourse would be 3 or 4 day racing, now he'd keep the horses and while the races.

This is what I can gather now, because I left home when I was about 6 and I came over here and I didn't have that much contact with home, well I mean my mother was alive until 1945, course when I'd meet her, she'd be telling me bits of history, but I wasn't interested, remember I was pretty well walking in history, but anyway they'd have about 9 or 10 racehorses, that'd mean they'd get in 3 or 4 local people, couple of servants for race week, as I said, it would last 3 weeks. At the end of the 3 weeks my father and grandfather etcetera they would take down the jumps and they'd store them until the races the following. So for them it was fairly big business you see. Now the last official one was about 1920, you had the Troubles in '20 and '21, that finished the Knockbarron Races, Pauline, as a big event.

Now another bunch of landlords in the area were the Smiths, they'd tie up with your parish, Smiths of Masonbrook. One of them was ancestor to Martyn of Tulira, Martyn of Tulira's mother was a Smith and when she married into the Martyns – they were landlords for barely 40 people – the Smiths were so delighted they said that she got her weight – as a dowry, she got her weight in money. She married Martyn. Now the Smiths were Catholic, they were reasonably big landlords, but they were fairly popular, but now they lasted until about 1932 or '3, and there was a big row around that period in Loughrea and I often think about it. Smiths of Masonbrook now in its heyday when I left Loughrea, they had about 1000 acres of land, they had land in Masonbrook and I think they had land down towards Carra or that direction, now they'd have about 25 workers, they'd have seasonal workers you see, they'd have a lot of tillage, they'd have turnips, potatoes, they'd have corn, they'd have about 600 sheep, possibly about five or six hundred cattle, and they were the main source of employment, they and works in Ballydougan, in the '20s and further back. Now Smiths would have about 25 workers all year round, then during the turnip-thinning season, mangold-thinning, weeding, they'd employ local youngsters, women. I remember now seeing local women working in it, you know, they'd work for a couple of weeks. They were pretty good employers.

But anyway they got involved in 1932 in what was a stupid row really, at the time there was a doctor in Loughrea called Dr Ryan. He was a distant relation to my father's, one of these old-time doctors of course, who was a good doctor, everybody liked him, he wasn't – you know, he never charged a fee – often got money, often didn't, but he had a big family, I think he had about 15 or 16 of a family, and his eldest son was educated in Trinity. Now Dr. Ryan died suddenly in the 30s, of course he was the dispensary doctor, which was a good job at the time. Now even though of course he had a fairly good job, he had a big family, he wasn't rich by any means, anyway 'twas suggested that his son would get the job here, just qualified from Trinity, and he couldn't get it, because at the time a doctor educated in Trinity would be looked on with suspicion you see. Might be a modern, you know what I mean like, and the bishop refused – well the bishop was only obeying the law you know – the bishop refused to sanction Dr Ryan. There was – immediately Pauline, there was murder, the town went on strike and everyone went fighting for Dr Ryan, and they brought a – the appointment was given to a doctor, I forget his name, he didn't stay in Loughrea a week, they ran him out of it.

Then the Smiths got involved somehow and they backed up the Ryans, and in one year Masonbrook went like a house of cards, the land was divided, the family – James Smith died, the head of the family, his wife left and went to live down near Kilreekil, she had a farm of land in it, and they were gone like that! Masonbrook was gone, the house was knocked and the land was divided. It was a stupid row, you see, now it was their father built – gave the land for building, the cathedral in Loughrea and he gave money for it, and it must have been a terrible blow for them, you know, to lose all their property, but that was the law – eventually the thing settled down, Pauline, and the doctor was appointed, that was the finish of Smiths and their connection with Martyn of Tulira.

Now another – the only family left there that were landlords in my time are the Burkes of Ballydougan, and they're hereditary, Pauline, for the simple reason that they're Protestant, and back around some time in the 19th century, when the local priest wanted to build a church in the parish of Ballydougan, he asked another family who had a fairly large farm of land, they were actually distant connections of my grandmother, Tullys, had a couple of hundred acres of land near Loughrea, and they were Catholics, and they wouldn't give a site to the priest, but he got a site from the Protestant Burkes, and when the church was consecrated and built, in his first sermon, he thanked the Burkes of Ballydougan for giving the land, he said, 'there'll be Burkes in Ballydougan', he said, 'when there won't be a Tully in the place'. There's still Burkes in Ballydougan Pauline, the Tullys are long gone.

Now the Tullys are another interesting family, some of them settled in Australia and became big landowners out there, and they were involved in land wars up in Woodford and now they were famous characters. Now that was the Burkes. Now down the road there was a smaller, Hardys, in Dartfield, they had a couple of hundred acres of land, they went off to Dublin, some of their descendants are still around. You had Harry Ussher then down below Loughrea who had racehorses at the Galway Races in the 1930s and 40s. They're gone, of course, too.

Then my father died, Pauline, around 1927. Now he went to a fair in Loughrea, he was only about 41 years of age and he never came back. He never came home from the fair, Pauline. You see he hadn't been well for a couple of weeks before, and this particular morning he had pigs to sell. Now we were close to Loughrea, it was less than a mile he'd be walking the pigs as far as I remember. I remember the morning now he walked the pigs into the fair, but he wasn't well, and mother tried to stop him from going, but he went and he sold the pigs and he never came back, he got a – pain. They sent for an old doctor who was in Loughrea, a resident doctor, and sure he gave him the wrong treatment. Dr Ryan was in business at the time and by the time they got to Dr Ryan, Dr Ryan diagnosed an appendix burst. And he died. I never saw him again. So he was buried on the 8th of December 1926. For about three or four months after he was gone, I'd be going looking for him now you see, looking what happened him –

PAULINE: *What age were you about?*

1927, I was born in '20, by about early January '27, anyway my mother wrote here to my uncle who was living here, who was also from east Galway, and she said she was having a terrible time, so he went over on a horse and sidecar and he brought me back and I remember that day now too, I was about six when I came, anyways. It was a long trip, Pauline, back from Loughrea on a horse and sidecar, about a four-hour trip, now I was coming along from Loughrea to Gort, again I was looking at history but didn't realize it, the landlords were going, most of them had gone, Persses had just left Roxborough, and people were moving down from the hills like Kilnedeema and Boherbuoy, to new holdings along Castledaly, along Kilchreest.

Previously, say two years before that, there would be no houses from Kilchreest to Gort, only two or three Persse houses, all the land belonged to the Persses of course, and the Lahans. The Lahans are still there, actually, in Cloone, and the Galbraiths in Peterswell they're gone too, and the Dalys in Castledaly they're still around something, they were all small landlords, but anyway I came, Pauline, the last thing my uncle said when he left when I said goodbye [*to my mother*], he said, 'don't be one bit surprised I could be back again tomorrow'. I'm still here, Pauline, that's how I came here. I suppose I got to like the place, Pauline, for the simple reason you see there were 3 or 4 women living next door and they had no kids. I had a wonderful time with all these old ladies spoiling me. I was really spoiled you know, so then my uncle and aunt, they had no kids so you can imagine, it was the life of Reilly.

Anyway I went to school, Pauline, around May 1927. The first day I went to school there was a girl from Carron down there brought me to school, she was McNamara, and I got on reasonably well at school, it helped me at school because they had a new teacher in the school, it was the first. Up to 1927 it was a one-teacher school and there was up to 60 or 70 pupils, one teacher to teach. They were after getting a teacher who happened to be from Loughrea, where I came from, so again I was in clover. School in my time, there was always a bully or two knocking around, because you had a slightly different accent you know, there was only one or two bullies, most of the rest of the kids were nice and friendly, but there was always a few of them, and Irish had just begun to come in, and I didn't like Irish that much, but we got through it, and I spent seven years going to ... There were 60 pupils, over 60, when I first, the first day I went going to that school in 1927. When I left eight years afterwards it was down to 26. But there it stopped, it began to build up again. That'll tell you, it will give you an idea of what emigration, low marriages say from '26 to '32, and '33, which were the years of the Depression, you know, there was trouble all over the world, financial problems. That was interesting enough, we had our ups and downs, and then of course, with all the …

Usually when I'd come home from school in the evening my grand-aunt was alive, she'd have a huge pan of potatoes and rashers, she'd have enough for four people, I'd take about two mouthfuls. She died about – there was a bad flu about 1934, it finished a lot of the old people, my grandaunt who was 84, and that was a real bad flu, hardly anybody got the doctors, of course, but it killed a lot of the old people. And I left school, of course, delighted to leave school at the age of 14, and went working on a farm doing this, that and the other thing, and still here.

PAULINE: *And where did you work?*

Ah sure around the farm – then by the time I was 12, I used to go back every year to my mother, footing turf, saving hay, from the age of 12 until 1945 I used to go back, leave home twice a year with a horse or a pair of horses, go back say in July, say cutting hay, bring home the turf, didn't have any tillage until 1941, so it wasn't too bad. 1941 my mother had to start ploughing up land that wasn't fit for ploughing, it was only fit for grazing cattle and sheep, and a lot of people in east Galway hadn't a tillage tradition, you know. They had to plough up some of the finest land in Ireland and the corn was never reaped, the land was often too rich. But up to 1945, Pauline, I'd leave here about 8 o'clock in the evening and arrive home about 12 o'clock that night, with a pair of horses, the following morning I'd go down to the bog in Carra or out ploughing.

Finally the war finished in 1945. My mother died in 1945, and I had one sister by the way, and I forgot to mention I had two step-sisters and a step-brother, they went to America in about 1927 – and one of them's still alive, you know. My father was married twice, Pauline, I should have mentioned that originally. Actually my father's first wife, there's a nice story told about her. During one of the race days in Knockbarron round about 1917 or '18, all in the house were gone to the races, they were only across the road anyway, and when they were gone, this big travelling man came in, a Traveller, and he demanded money off her, and he demanded a slitch which is of bacon, of course, hanging up in the kitchen. They'd kill a couple of pigs always for the races, and kill a sheep or two, I believe. Anyway he demanded meat off her, and he demanded money, so she said that the money, she'd have to go up and there was a little loft, it was a long, low, thatched house when I left it in 1927 – it's long ago gone, of course – 'the money is left up there', she said. 'I'll have to get it', so she stepped up and she whipped out a double-barrelled shotgun at him, and pointed it at him, and he ran [*laughs*]. He didn't look for any more money. She died then, about 1917 or '18, I don't know what happened her, and she left two girls and a boy, they went to America, they never came home. My stepbrother came home once, he died last year. I suppose that's about the sum total. My mother then died in '45. I had one sister, she joined the nuns in England, and she died about two years ago, and I stayed here then, until I met her ladyship.

PAULINE: *And what happened the land in Loughrea?*

We sold it, Pauline, and my sister got the dowry going into the nuns, so she was quite happy in the nuns and she had a good old life over there. She went to England, she finished up in an interesting convent, she died only there a few years ago. This convent belonged to the last of Napoleon's wives, you know Napoleon Bonaparte and all his crowd, one of the Napoleons he was emperor about 1884, and they were beaten – he was well out of France, and he had one son who was heir to the throne, but the son was killed in the war, by an accident, and the mother was heartbroken, so she had to leave France and she came to live in England, and they gave her a little house, Pauline, big enough for about 500 people. It's a big mansion, big palace, it's a beautiful residence, and it fell into the possession of the nuns around, before 1900, and one of the most famous nuns in that area, she was in it when I went out in 1948 to my sister's first profession, she's from Ballinasloe actually, Mother Rowntree. She was a character really, she wasn't a Reverend Mother, she was Queen of England, yeah, you know. At the time she had about 100 Protestant girls going to school there, most of them were children of big shots in England, as well as the Roman Catholics. It's a public school now and the nuns are nearly all gone, but they had their own, they had about 100 cows. The land is all divided now and built over, so it was an interesting place my sister finished up, you know. Most of the nuns of course were Irish. They're down to about 7 or 8 nuns now, Farnborough Hill as it's called.

PAULINE: *And where did you meet Ann?*

Well I met her at the carnival in Gort, although she was living near enough to me. I suppose I met her at the carnival officially for the first time, she wasn't far away, just half a mile across the fields. Co. Clare is only about over there you see, a short distance away. They had chair-o-planes and that kind of thing, and they'd have a dance probably in the town hall later on. That was great fun, Pauline, because everyone went to the carnival, you know, you had the chair-o-planes, you had the throwing the rings and trick of the loops – behind Josie Mack's, in Gort. There aren't many left that were at that carnival, you know. I was counting them the other night, the people that went to school with me. There are about 7 left, the people who went to school with me in

1927. Of course, one of the big things when I was growing up if you wanted to enter into the criminal element was robbing orchards you know, that was about the only big-time crime you could –

PAULINE: *And were there many orchards around?*

There was two – there was quite a few actually. One of the most unusual orchards was a family by the name of Spelman. They had a huge orchard of plums which they used to pick every year and they were shipped away – I don't know where. A couple of weeks, you know, it was a big business. I think it's all gone. There was quite a lot of big orchards, nearly everybody had a few trees, apples were a big part of farming life that time. I remember a family up there. They used have a pit of apples and they'd sell them in Ennis and Galway afterwards, but we had an orchard in the village which had two apple trees, but they were the most beautiful apples you ever ate. I raided them with a pal twice, and each time – the first time, it cured us of orchard robbing for quite a long time, the two trees – the two trees were quite close to the house. There was an elderly woman in the house at the time, and her granddaughter, and she had two sons, now they'd normally be gone at night time, you know, but we decided this Friday night anyway, with a pal of mine, I was about 14 at the time, he was younger, he's still alive, but we decided to try. It was well-fenced you see, there was barbed wire on one side, a big hedge, and close to the house then and it was pretty hard to get in there without being caught. Now we knew the two men of the house would be gone, and the old woman would go to bed reasonably early and her grandchild would also probably be gone to bed. We tried about 10 o'clock one night anyway, it was a Friday night, and what I did I was wearing a long trousers, tied here you see [*at the ankles*] and slipped the apples down inside. He climbed up the tree, now we tried it twice, so I'd better not mix them. The first time anyway we got away successfully, and we came back home with, I suppose, we'd have a half-stone weight of apples, lovely apples, came back home around half-ten, quarter to eleven, and we divided the apples, and I hid apples in our hayshed, which is still up there, and he was next door, he was staying with an aunt next door, he had his. We came home from school – yeah I was still going to school – came home from school the following evening. The village was crawling with guards and everything, Jesus Mary and Joseph tonight, we didn't know why till I went in home and Kevin next door, ran in, 'Jees Tommie', he said, 'the house is full of guards abroad'. We put two and two together – I'll never forget it, Pauline, as long as I live – we nearly died, we waited all the evening and wondering when the guards would come for us and waited till about eleven o'clock at night, we took the apples and we threw them in holes above in the rocks. Sure about two days later we discovered that the guards had nothing at all to do with the apples. We went to find the apples but sure they were all eaten by crows. It was a distinctly different matter.

About two years later I tried the orchard again with another fellow, and that time, the next time we tried it the fellow who was with me was about 18, and I was 16, everything went grand. He was up in the tree and he'd be handing the apples down to me, and I had the same plan again. Now we knew also it'd be the same routine, the men'd be away. This was a Monday, he'd be gone to the shop. It was about ten o'clock. Jesus! Lo and behold he's up in the tree, we're just going grand, we heard footsteps, you see there was a path coming from the orchard, as we called it, to the shop, it's actually one of the oldest roads in Ireland, that time, now it's covered in bushes, we heard steps coming, and I said, 'Mikey' – Mikey is dead now – 'be quiet', said I, 'he won't know where you are'. Now Mikey stayed quiet, you see, first of all, the man came into the front of the old house – at this time now they had a new house, the old house was still there, but they had moved a little bit further away from the trees, not very far, they were still in full view of the apple trees – he came into the old yard where the old house was and he opened the little gate and closed it. Now he came along in our direction and there was another little wicket. And as soon as he left his hand on the gate your man jumped out of the tree. If he stayed quiet! Nothing for it but go through the hedge, a briar hedge with the barbed wire on it, we got out through it and I still having the apples and we ran across country for about a mile – he followed us you know – but we don't know, because he always had a gun, and he wouldn't be shy of using it, we don't know whether he went in for a gun or not. I think he did, but I'm not sure, but anyway we ran for about three-quarters of a mile eventually. That was the end of the orchard raiding [*laughter*].

PAULINE: *Seriously though, wasn't it, you were stealing apples, their livelihood.*

Sure, apples around Christmas that time were wonderful. Some people would preserve them in hay until the following February and March.

PAULINE: *They'd make jam with them or cakes –*

I made crabapple jelly. There were a lot of crabs around, Pauline, they're nearly all gone now, but there was a friend of mine, Pauline, working up in Marble Hill, not long dead now too, he was a tradesman, and there was a big orchard up in Marble Hill, these now were the Burkes of Marble Hill. They were the same Burkes we'd have back where I come from.

PAULINE: *Where is Marble Hill?*

Up Derrybrien, east Galway, towards Woodford, they were big landlords, Pauline, and they were a mixed lot too, they were Catholic and Protestant, etc. We'll go back to that again. Anyway, two fellows, they got a job in Marble Hill, I think it was building a house. Now at this stage, Pauline, the Burkes were nearly gone. Their descendants were still there but they hadn't big, they're not big landlords anymore. But anyway, they were building a house, they discovered this orchard which belonged to Burkes of Marble Hill, huge wall around it, and hard to get into it. Anyway, Friday night they made a little ladder, and they had to walk up for miles to the orchard and they brought a bag with them. And they succeeded in getting in to the orchard, and they picked up three or four stone of apples, Pauline, and put them in a bag, got out of the orchard and came back home. Now they were scratched, you see, because the wall was full of bushes and briars, the apple trees some of them had bushes growing up through them, but they got their apples anyway. They came back anyway to wherever they were staying. I think they were staying in an old house, and they put the apples in a bag, and they left them up in a kind of a – there was a kind of an old outhouse joined on the house, or a barn, they left the apples in it, left them up in a box or something. Went off to work Saturday morning, came back Saturday evening, they'd be going home Saturday evening – someone had broken in and eat every one of their apples. After all their trouble [*Laughs*].

Anyway, they found a set of vestments in Marble Hill some years ago. They reckoned they were two or three hundred years old, hid during the penal days, I think they were in good condition too – hid in a fairly safe place. I don't know what became of them. Because they have vestments in Loughrea, Pauline, sent by the French government, you know, after the Battle of Aughrim. St Ruth was killed at the Battle of Aughrim, and he was buried in Loughrea. Now unfortunately they don't know where he was buried, he was buried in the Abbey grounds, there's no headstone or anything. But in thanksgiving to the people of Loughrea for looking after him they sent a set of vestments, lovely vestments, to the Loughrea parish priest later on. They're still in Loughrea now. They have a little museum in Loughrea attached to the Church. And there's a set of banners in the church in Loughrea which Robert Gregory designed. Wait a minute now. Was it Robert Gregory? Was it Jack B Yeats? A beautiful set of banners that you'd use in Benediction, handmade, Pauline, priceless. It was Robert Gregory designed them or else Jack B Yeats. Now remember they were Protestant. And they were in Loughrea – one of the nuns showed them to me. They're worth seeing and photographing.

PAULINE: *What's the biggest change you see in the area over the last fifty years?*

Oh sure, wait till I see, there's so many changes, fifty or sixty years ago having a bicycle was a big thing ... You see, 1917, '18, '19 were good years, and a lot of people were able to build good houses. For instance, 1918–19, Kilboys in Loughrea they were making sidecars. They were able to sell at the height – my father bought a sidecar about 1918–19. The big thing, Pauline, would be to have a horse and side-car or a horse and trap, a big lift-up. What was the biggest change? Farming up to 1930 they were using mainly scythes. There was a man up the road made his living cutting hay with the scythe, and Annie remembers as well as I do, and he cut corn, he cut wheat with the hook, he cut an acre of hay with the scythe for about half a crown, that's in the 1930s, then the mowing machine was a big step forward for cutting the hay, then after the mowing machine you had the reaper and binder, then, of course, you went on the combine harvester, they were all steps in the chain.

Then, of course, the fact that people began to get a little bit of education, because there was no secondary school when I left school. I left about 1935, to my knowledge there was no secondary school. There was a school in Loughrea all right, Pauline. It seems the parish priest in Gort sometime in 1915–16, Christian Brothers suggested opening a school in Gort, but he stopped it! So I've been told, now, we had a private secondary school in the late '30s, small one, it lasted for a few years, then the Tech of course opened. The fellows who went to school with me, Pauline, they didn't get to see any secondary education. Some of the girls went to the convent all right, in Anna's time the Tech opened that was where everybody went. That was a big step. They got a chance to continue the little bit of education, read and write, and learn domestic economy. The teacher in our school as well as teaching catechism and everything else she also taught sewing, Pauline, sewing and knitting, you know, and girls got a pretty good grounding in the ordinary National school. Then, of course, emigration started, people instead of staying began to move, you know, to America, '26, '7, they didn't go to England – seasonal workers, from Connemara and Mayo, they used to go to England back to 1900, they'd go over in April come back in October. There was a man in the village, I knew his son, he used to go to England every year. He had about 13 or 14 kids here at home, stuck there in one of the old houses. Now he'd go to England in April and he'd come back the following October, he'd take the train from Gort to Cork and cross to England. He had been in the British

Army, so he would know his way around, now he'd come back in October, back in by train to Gort, and coming home, Pauline, he'd have about 30 or 40 pairs of boots – there was no shoes that time – hung over his shoulder, and a big fletch of American bacon, which was a fletch of bacon about three or four feet long, must have been some scenery – that went on, Pauline, till about the First World War. Now there were 15 in that family, there's one left in Ireland, he never married. They're in America. That was what you'd call seasonal migration, but a lot of workers, in fact I was up in my 20s when we'd have Connemara workers coming around digging the potatoes, and they'd be Irish speakers, you know. They wouldn't pretend to know any English, you know. They'd come around in October and they'd work, a lot of them, you'd see them at Mass on Sunday up here and they'd be talking Irish.

Another change is, the youngsters, they'd be wearing short trousers till they were 16, they'd get the long trousers. The girls began to get a bit more modern, you know. The women were losing the shawls, there were women using shawls till well into the 40s, but very few at that stage. Then you see, Pauline, the days of the small farmer began to, shall we say – in the 40s and 50s it wasn't as easy for a small farmer to get a wife as it would be fifty years before that, because maybe one of the girls had gone to England or America and she'd write to the sister saying 'why don't you come out here'.

Another change. Let's say women began to come out – they were prisoners to a certain extent all their life – that was a big step for them to be able to … The dancehalls, some priests cursed them, and actually I heard one priest cursing the dancehall from the altar, while another priest was building one over the road.

That was a big step because for the first time people from different parishes could meet. Because life in Ireland was very parochial, Pauline, and people would say if you wanted a wife get one from your own parish. But from the 1940s people were beginning to come in from ten miles, that was another big change, you were beginning to realize that Ireland was a little bit bigger than your own parish.

Then, of course, the cinema came which was cursed. The cinema was great, I loved the cinema, because for the first time you weren't, say … I could always read, I was happy with books, but other fellows who didn't want to read and couldn't, the cinema was great for them.

20 February 2004

I was born in Dublin. But I suppose I should start off with how we first came to Tulira. Tulira is lastingly famous for Edward Martyn who lived here for all of his life from the time he was about 20, 25, or so, when he came back from Oxford, and he lived at Tulira, and he did all these very famous things which you don't want me to talk about now – when he died, the place was left to my grandmother, entailed on her, and she was the last to the Martyns. Her father was Edward Martyn's father's younger brother. She would have been a niece of Edward Martyn – no I'm wrong, now, she would have been a first cousin. Then it came down from my grandmother to my father, and to me.

So, then having designed the house and built it, they then built it to extraordinary specifications. I mean it's all cut stone the whole way around, makes it look like Lough Cutra or any of these castles around the country, and John Betjeman who was later Poet Laureate in England and was a great friend of my mother, he used to stay there regularly, and he said it was probably one of the finest pieces of Victorian architecture – Victorian domestic architecture – that he knew, which is quite interesting. But anyhow they built a house where everything that looks like marble, unlike in a lot of Victorian houses, is in fact marble, all the different coloured marbles, they're all in the hall, all round the hall, and they did everything literally to the highest possible specifications. And then, when it was all done, my grandmother always used to say, that they scarcely bothered to furnish the house, heat it, and he only did it very quickly and became a sort of recluse and retired to live in the tower room, almost in a monastic way, and that's where he lived, in his early days he used to hunt in Leicestershire, and then he came back, but I don't think he ever did very much hunting at all. That's Edward Martyn, he never married. By the time my grandmother who was left it, from then until my father got married and I came to live there as well, there was about seven or eight years during which, once again, it was totally empty without any heating, without anything at all. So that didn't help it much. Then it went through all the rest of those years up until 19 – my mother left in 1940 – odd, during the 40s, again, it never had very much done to it, because my mother couldn't afford it and money wasn't forthcoming generally and one thing and another so it got sort of – semi-abandoned, and then after we left, I used to come down once every year for about three weeks with my grandmother, and we'd stay there for about – no a couple of months, I think. And again nothing would be done at all, the gardens were kept by a couple of men, that's about all. Then, we got married in 1952, I suppose I should go over my life a bit before that, possibly. I lived at Tulira, and when I went to – I didn't go to school until I was 12.

PAULINE: *So what did you do before that, tutor?*

I had – the first person to look after me after I had Nanny and all that sort of thing would have been almost a relation of Shane's I think, Maura Quinn, who would be what to you –

PAULINE: *An aunt-in-law –*

And she looked after me, and I used to be taken out and I used be left in the woods, to play with a sort of elephant thing I had, and we'd be walking, up to the rockery, and here would be this man waiting, and of course 'twas Frank Quinn, so they'd go off in a hullaballoo, and I was left to play on my own! (big laugh) Oh that's quite true. That was the elephant. That all went quite well, and she went off and got married and had, I think, 21 children, one of whom was recently mayor of Galway, another of whom is a top banker in New York, and Maura died some years ago. Then after Maura I got a governess from, she came from Trim, called Miss Harlan, and she used to teach me. But my mother was American, and she had sort of very fancy ideas, so after breakfast it was essential that I went out and got fresh air, and exercise, and then I would come in and have my lessons. So it didn't take me long to wangle that if I got far enough away it would shorten the lessons. So I used to get up the woods as far as I could, spent the day shouting and screaming, they had a big bell, and this bell, they'd ring the bell like mad, and eventually I'd come and of course when I did come a good bit of time was wasted chasing around the table with a ruler (laughs) My education was very scant and that time, but I wanted to read, and so I did, and I also wanted to be able to add up, so I did. And I read an awful lot, my mother had a very big library in Tulira, so I was used to reading and I enjoyed reading and I was encouraged, so I read a great deal. So I then went off at the age of 12, to day school in Dublin, called some convent, I was meant to be going off to – my father was in Downside in Somerset and I was meant to be going there to the prep school, and the war began. Just when I'd got over there, got my uniform, and come back, they declared war, the beginning of September, so I had about a year more with the governess, and then I went to a Dublin day school. I was used to being in the woods, and couldn't see the point – I used to arrive late in school, this fellow had a strap, the headmaster, held out your hand, you got two or three or four, so I arrived in late every single day, and of course my hands got as hard as you like. Then the next trick was to go into class and be asked to write something, 'very sorry sir my hands are too sore' [*laughs*] so they didn't have much success with me. So I was in that school, and it wasn't practical for me to be in Dublin and one thing and another, I went to Glenstal in Limerick, the Benedictine monks in Limerick, and I had a great time there, and I was really beginning to enjoy that, when my father – suddenly the European war ended, and my father announced to me one morning, 'You're going to Downside next term', and I'd left all my stuff and everything in Glenstal, and I was just going to be a prefect, and life was really sailing. So I was whipped out of that, and sent to Downside, so I had two years in Downside which I really enjoyed, and had a great time, and then I did all those various certificates for getting into university, and having left school, Downside, again I was mad keen in those days – in those days everybody was mad crazy on the war, and we all wanted to go into the OTC the JTC – Junior Training Corps, so we were mad crazy, the old boys used to come back, those who survived, and they'd be heroes, and everyone would want to know them, so we all, naturally – so what do you think happened to me, just in my last term at school, just as I'm going happily to war – bloody war ended! [*Laughs*]. I literally never did get over there, because it upset me terribly and wrecked my whole life at that stage, so then I got all bolshy, because there was conscription, so I got bolshy about that, I had no intention of going into an army, it wasn't much of an army, without a war, you know. And so anyway I didn't have to join up, 'I'm Irish', which of course was a great mistake because they all had a marvellous time, all the officers because if they didn't do anything, there was nothing to do, so they went shooting, hunting, fishing and racing, all at the expense of His Majesty, so I missed out on that, and all the camaraderie. And then when I took a what is now known as a gap year, so I went to Spain, I hunted for the winter, and I was living down in Waterford at that time, when my parents were divorced my mother married Villiers-Stuart, who came from a huge great house down in Waterford, and I lived there you see, unless I came to Tulira, right up until I left Oxford, quite a long time. When I was in Waterford I hunted a lot when I was down there, and that house was run on a lavish scale, butler, footman, cook, kitchenmaids, God knows how many, it was a huge house, bigger than Tulira.

PAULINE: *Did your mother have any more children?*

No. I had a stepbrother, if you like, no relation, he was my stepfather's son, so we were always great friends and still are, to this day. I lived there, then, and then the summer I went to Spain, to Madrid, got digs there, and got myself down to the coast, and that was before all that coastal development, it was quite interesting, just after the war, and it hadn't really recovered from the Spanish Civil War, and all the beaches now they're all the Costa Brava, were all cobbled, there was no sand there at all, and it was all barren countryside, except for marshy bits, just generally had a very good time, bullfights and all sorts, I can understand Spanish a bit you know. The following year I went to Oxford where I spent three years reading law, which I took a degree in, then went and worked for a very short space of time in the City, banking, then, instead of doing the law. I wanted to do the law very much. So what do you think happened to me then? I wanted to get married, so as matter of interest that was 52 years ago, so being determined to do that, I did. We had no money you see, and in those days if you went to be a barrister you spent a good few years before you got anything, and it really would cost you money, so I went to the City and worked in the City banking. So I then got very ill after we were married and then came back here to convalesce, and Ann and I came to Tulira for convalescence [*laughs*]. The place was falling down now, and the whole of the, what they now call, they call the east wing, in my day it was called the nursery wing, it was absolutely it was all rooks and nettles, had all collapsed, come down on that side. We had

John Gaffney came to work as a sort of, you know, by the hour, by the day kind of thing, he wasn't actually working for me, with me, also Lowry Murray. So he came along, now he had the advantage of being an electrician, and he was also a plumber, this was John Gaffney, and he a better than average carpenter as well, so there was nothing he couldn't do. So he took on John Murray, Lowry Murray, a very young man, he was about my – I mean at the time I was only about 24, Lowry was about 4 years younger than me. So anyhow, we all worked at it, and there was no electric light in the house, and there were only about two working bathrooms, pumps didn't work, wells didn't work, there was an old diesel pump that used work when I was a boy, they pumped the water out of the well for the horse, and the horse would tow it round and round and round in a circle for about two hours, and that would fill up the tanks, huge tanks. That well had packed up, I think, and in my mother's day there would have been a tiny diesel engine, and that's all there was. So anyway we gradually got it going. There was virtually no land in Tulira either, that got taken away during – whenever Edward Martyn died, he left a very magnanimous will leaving all sorts of things everywhere, he left a lot of money to the Gaelic League, to Sinn Fein, to various funds, all over the show, so in actual fact, his will was bankrupt, and so my grandmother turned the whole thing over to the Land Commission, and paid off the endowments for all the lands sold, and then she bought the place back from the Land Commission, but in doing so, she was a woman and not very knowledgeable about that sort of thing, and also she had a huge place in Suffolk, and a place called Bridewell, near Tuam, that was a very old place, belonged to the family called Kirwans who were one of the twelve tribes of Galway, and she inherited that place, so that was enough land, but in buying it back from the Land Commission it was a tragedy, because there was no longer enough land to maintain the place, I mean, no way would it. In fact the way it was sliced we managed to collect the worst off, as well. And also they had a lot of indebtness with the land, and so that was, when we came I was obviously very keen. My father told me I could certainly have it and he gave me the place, and someone said when are we going to come back, come back now, otherwise it will be gone. So we got literally a man and a dog and a stick and a cock of hay, one cow, it was pretty desperate. So we started off with a garden, trying to make a market garden. And in those days in Galway believe it or not we sold heads of lettuce, turnips, cabbage.

Anyway about that time when we'd first come – I'll go back to the electrics problem – when we came back to live there, we had candles, lamps and not one bit of electricity, and it had always been my ambition when I was a boy, at Tulira, two things I really saw missing and I saw other places coming up with, particularly Ballydougan and Rockfield and all these smart places, I was always very anxious that we should have it. Immediately when we got the place I went to the ESB. My mother had turned them down earlier on the rural electrification scheme, and we were the only place in the parish that hadn't accepted the rural electrification, and a lot of houses then had got only one bulb, you know, got the wire up to the house and one bulb, and that was it, and they kind of resented it in the early days, you know, they didn't really want it, but they didn't want to be seen without it either! So many of them literally had only got one bulb, I used to study this in great detail. So I went to the ESB and explained to them, but in the end they really wanted to get the light in, so we literally had it strung up to the door and virtually nothing else, and then John Gaffney and Lowry Murray and myself got stringing wires all over the place, all over Tulira, we kept on stringing them, and they never changed the floor or anything. So anyway the other exciting thing about the lights, when Ann and I came back, and at this stage our eldest daughter, Angela she was called, we'd left London, and we'd spent the Christmas before with Ann's parents in Clounee, Ballinrobe – a lovely house on the shores of Lough Carra, and we also spent a bit of time in Dublin in my grandmother's place, so in January we came down to Tulira, the plan was the ESB knew we were coming, and as we drove into the yard, they switched the lights on, and that appeared in the *Tribune,* at the time, 'Lights in castle for first time'. That was great fun. But as I say there weren't many lights. But then as we went on the electrification, the walls were so thick, and in those days if you wanted central heating in there were huge big pipes, enormous big pipes right through. So that didn't exist, and also they have better drills now than they had then. Gradually then so as to get the heat – we used to have log fires all over, and plenty of timber, we were crazy, we used to have one person just literally barrowing timber in all day, and we had a huge fire in the hall, and in the rooms downstairs and even with all that – and when I was a boy we used have fire in the bedrooms, fires all over the place. Then we put in the heating, because we decided the more electricity we used, the cheaper it was. Everything became electric, we had electric tubular heating, but at that time it was quite effective. Then the other thing we had to do – the avenue I forgot to mention were always terrible pot-holes, literally couldn't drive down it, and when the place had been divided they'd taken the main avenue away, the gates were still there, so that what we were using was literally a farm road, it came out by Murrays' house ... And my mother had got gates from Cregclare, quite nice gates, and we brought the gates from Dunsandle, to Tulira, they're beautiful gates. And we carried on living there then, and we were very interested in hunting, almost immediately, well we left it a year or two before we got into the hunting, and the first thing we started off was to try and get the garden going and the worst thing of all was when we did get going, quite well with turnips and lettuce and so on, the only snag was, the person we supplied most to, went broke, and didn't pay us at all. So we gave up the market gardening and it wasn't till quite a few years later that we bothered to get the garden going. Then – there was no land to keep the place going and also we weren't sure if we were going to be able to manage the place because it looked a bit too far gone for us to really get after it, so we bought, or Grandmother bought for me, Rinville, and there was a smaller house there, and we moved in there. So it took us ages, really to get any kind of – then I got interested in machinery, we were going to do a bit of contracting work, so for years we did quite well from that, it started from a combine seed-driller, we got from Massey-Ferguson, we had a Massey-Ferguson tractor, we got that from old Tom Ruane in Castlebrien, and we got this combined seed and fertiliser drill.

Well I'll get back to Edward Martyn. When he left Oxford he went to Paris for a while, he used to go with a cousin of his called George Moore, George Moore was a great writer, and they were very much – they were always bickering with each other, you know, and had a tremendous sort of repartee, but for all that they were very fond of each other. George Moore was a great artist as well, and they went to Paris and they bought all these paintings, literally from the artists at the time, and among them he had a Renoir, Degas, Cezanne, Monet, unbelievable, he had a very large collection, and they were all left to between the Municipal Art Gallery and the National Gallery. So none of those came to us.

PAULINE: *Why didn't he leave them [to you]?*

That's a very good question. I told you that he never got married, and a lot of people have thought, there has been a suggestion, that he might have been a little bit on the homosexual side, but in actual fact, that doesn't appear to be true, there is no evidence at all for that. But on the other hand he definitely was a misogynist, in other words a woman-hater, but that doesn't mean he was a man-lover. When he found out that he had nobody to leave the place to, that it had to be entailed on a woman – my grandmother – that was a bit of a blow! But he had to leave the place to her, because it was entailed, direct line. He was so upset by that that he was quite determined to leave everything everywhere, even the big fireplace in the Hall was left, and the one in the dining-room – and it would have wrecked the house – they were left to the Carmelite monastery in Clarendon St, in Dublin, and they didn't take them, very nicely. He also left the entire library – and they had a wonderful library, but the Martyn library we never got because it was left to the Carmelite monastery, and that was an enclosed monastery at the time, but nobody was allowed into it, so nobody could go in to the library, members of the family were supposed to be allowed to go in, my father did once, apparently. But anyway, time went on, and an American nun who was doing a thesis, one way or another got access – oh, no sorry, she didn't, she tried to, she failed. And somebody else, a man, doing some similar thing, a lot of people, students, he picked to do some stuff, you know, and they wanted to get at the library, and he arrived into the library, and they said, there was a sort of what they call lay-brother looking after the library, and this fellow said he wanted to look at Edward Martyn's bequest, and so he said, 'never heard of him'. So the other man said, 'would anyone know?', he hadn't been there long, the other man asked, 'would anyone else know?', and 'ah I wouldn't think so', he said, 'the library had all been redone, the whole thing, reorganized there a few years ago, and all I do know', he said, 'is that there was a tremendous amount of dirty stuff, it was all thrown away and burnt'. Quite likely that some valuables were fairly dirty, and that seems to have been their fate. Very sad. The paintings on the other hand, quite a lot of them were left in storage and never taken out, very sad story as well, and some of them had been lent to my father, and when we had a sale in Tulira many years later, next thing somebody comes along from one of the National Gallery, Municipal Art Gallery, and they collected the paintings. And they'd been on loan to my father for – but I didn't know – for – and there had never been a word from the Gallery, they'd been on loan for, oh, about that time forty years. More, fifty. We had absolute chaos at the auction, obviously [*laughs*]. Anyway all that was all very sad, and I talked about buying the land back, and when the house was bought back again of course there wasn't much furnishing, and as I said earlier Edward Martyn had never fully furnished the new house. But when the estate became bankrupt from the point of view of the legacies, whereas I suppose my grandmother could have I suppose paid the legacies and kept her bit, but instead of that she chose to turn the whole thing in.

Then, the furniture was all sold again, that time, and there again my grandmother bought back the dining room table, the sideboard, and then she in turn furnished it from Oxford, and then by the time we got there just a few things, four-poster beds, Pugin furniture in the library some of which is now back there, and otherwise not much. That's the furniture.

The home farm at Cregclare was straight across the road from Tulira, then on the other side, all up to Derrybrien. When we came, we had about 220 acres with the castle. And then I bought a bit more. When we sold it there was about 250. [*My family came*] with Strongbow, a captain with Strongbow's army in 1170. So if you're wondering that I'm English [*laughs*] – Norman. He got out at the end of the war, they got a big allotment of land, before they got the land, they became merchants in Galway, and they had land all around the job, they spread around and they came to Dunguaire in Kinvara which was set up by the O'Flahertys, so they kept it. So Richard Martyn from Dunguaire married in the 16th century I think, 1500s, a Mrs Burke from Tulira, Tulira would have been built by the Burkes, the de Burgo family. Going back then to the estate that [*Edward Martyn*] was disappointed to leave to my grandmother, he was also disappointed – very proud of their religion, and that they were Catholic. They were granted this during the reign of Queen Anne, and they were allowed to keep their religion and their land in spite of the laws against Catholics. Most families had to change their religion in order to keep their land, but the Martyns were very strong Catholics, particularly if they were loyal to the king, but particularly if they were far away from London, because the king liked to have loyal groups, this happened in England – nearly always way up in the north of Scotland. So the Martyns were always very proud of that. So my grandmother, not only was she a woman, but she went off and she married a Presbyterian, and that was a disaster and very upsetting, for – but my father was brought up a Catholic and so was I.

PAULINE: *Would the Martyns have had a coal-mining claim in South Africa?*

No, we never had outside money coming in like that, they never married any heiresses, they never – well that's untrue because Edward Martyn's mother was an heiress, but the others were nearly all tribe members. But they had a lot of money because they were very rich merchants, huge land.

PAULINE: *Would you have liked Charles to have kept on Tulira?*

Well I think that comes later in the story, doesn't it. I suppose I'd better go on with the story a bit, hadn't I. You see the whole thing was a struggle to try and build it up, number one, and then to actually maintain it. And the place itself wasn't capable of producing anything till much later on when it did produce, so I tried all these things market gardening and so on, and then I moved into the machinery thing, and Tom Ruane said, 'Oh you'd get a grant for this', so I said 'Don't be silly why would they give me a grant', you see that was the first one in Galway that combined seed and fertiliser, and so anyway they said, well you have to sign a form, on the form it said, you have to hire a garage, so I said, I'm not going to sign that I'm not going to hire a garage, and he said, ah, just sign that I'll get you the grant, he was a sort of local politician you see, but then I got the idea of hiring it out and so I set off on my first expedition to do a job for somebody, and so we had the first combine harvester in Galway and a really amusing incident we had with the combine harvester, was that there was great rivalry between threshing and mills, the people at mills didn't like the idea of the combine harvester, much less than that, did they care for somebody like me going around taking money that maybe they could have, anyway I went on driving, so this particular day the combine went to start up, it was a wettish kind of a chilly morning we couldn't start til about eleven o'clock, the weather hadn't – put on the power, turned the key, nothing happened. So terrible trouble, it took us ages to find out what had happened, one of our rival friends had emptied a bag of sugar into the tank. It was a rotten thing, and slowed up the people who were cutting the corn, destroyed the whole fuel system got totally blocked up. But anyway we went on, and we did this contact work and that was quite successful and quite fun and Owen Linnane's son Eamon used to come and he used to drive it for me

PAULINE: *Used you drive it yourself?*

In the beginning I did all the time, and worked all the other things, I worked everything. That was what we did that and it worked quite well. Then we farmed we got a few pedigree herds of Aberdeen Angus cattle, but they wouldn't grow, the land wasn't that good – then we tried a bit of milk farming, that was another thing we tried, we tried dairy farming, but nobody did any dairy farming around Ardrahan, Dick Taylor had a few cows, and the next thing a few other people started too, and then we took it on ourselves to collect the milk, and we used go up every little boreen, they'd bring it to the top of the lane for us, and eventually we'd get them to the creamery ... So then we did oysters, we developed the oysters in Rinville, which we developed the oysters there, and they did very well, and then we sold the whole place for a very big profit. At that stage we thought when the oysters were going and the farm was going and the whole place was going, that that was the end of Tulira, and we did at that stage … but we started building it up again, and the hall, we painted the hall completely, when we went there all the plaster was coming down in the hall, and the halls were gone against the castle and against the staircase, so we had to build them all up new again. A lot of that we did ourselves and then some of it with some contractors, and – where'd it go next – we then moved into broilers, chickens, in the beginning it was fairly small, and then we'd sell them all privately, we had these houses, sell them at eight weeks, the stables were converted into hatcheries. We tried deep-litter eggs earlier. The broilers were great but we used have a terrible job, we had to kill them all. Then we met up with somebody who had hatcheries – we changed over, turned over onto hatchery supply. And that made us an enormous amount of money, really big money.

HOWLEY, Joe, late of Mervue (Sixth Anniversary). In loving memory of a great husband and father, who died 11th Sept 2005.
No longer in our lives to share, But in our hearts you are always there.
Loved and missed by your wife Madge, sons, daughters and extended family.
Anniversary Mass In Mervue Church 11th September at 12.30.

20 February 2004

PAULINE: *Where were you born?*

Granagh, Ardrahan; there were two brothers, and a sister, and one brother died and he's buried in the old cemetery in Ardrahan, the left-hand side of the gate as you go in. There's a Protestant half and a Catholic. He died from pneumonia, I think, he was only fourteen or fifteen months, but there was no cure for it that time. I went to school just straight across from my father's farm. The house is in Ardrahan, I was eight years there, I went to school in Peterswell, then I went to England. Pat Moylan taught me in Peterswell, Ciaran Moylan's father. I went to school with Ciaran, as a matter of fact. I was 14 leaving school, that was the time the beet started to come up, plenty of work there. They'd sow it in April with a turnip machine, we used a turnip machine that time, you'd make drills, but then they got very up-to-date after that, they were able to spray each side with the seed. There was a lot of feeding stuff, the tops of the beet you know and the pulp. It gave employment

PAULINE: *So did you leave home then, or did you stay in Ardrahan?*

I stayed then till 1944. Travelling around threshing, around Clare. I went to Dublin then, I was 9 years in Dublin, Artane, well, different parts but Artane I finished up in.

I was working on the buildings. Piece work making concrete blocks, was our job, 'twas hard work. You'd get more money than if you were working on flat time, you know. And, got married up there then

PAULINE: *Was she a Dublin lady?*

No. Tipperary. County. Got married in 1950 and we lived in Dublin till 1954. Came to Castletaylor. I got working with the Board of Works here in the town, had to cycle from Castletaylor to Galway, in and out every day, from June until the following March.

PAULINE: *How long would that take you to cycle?*

Ah 'twould depend on the weather, the breeze. Sometimes you'd have a tail back, 'twas getting quicker then. The one thing I did remember about it was, on this side of Clarinbridge, now, the Galway side, there was only one house in it at the time, Martin Burke's, and there was a field in it, and way off in the field every morning and I going in, I used to see this light in it, I'd be saying to myself, what is it, what is it, and I didn't have time (laughs) to investigate anyhow. This morning I was going in, I had the breeze to my back and I was making great time, I'll go over now till I see what this light is. Did you ever see one of these lanterns, with – there used to be bars around it to protect the glass, and on top on it, to keep the fox away from the ewes, an oil-lamp was it.

I'd leave Castletaylor about six o clock. Back about half-eight and nine o clock. I got the house here then, 1957, moved into here, into town.

PAULINE: *And do you remember any funny incidents in the house when you were young?*

There were, yeah, I remember one night in the bedroom that I used to sleep in, there were two beds in it that time, when you'd be in this bed you'd think that 'twas in that bed it was, when you'd be in this bed you'd think 'twas in the other bed, often we got – cousins slept when they came over, they'd think I'd be trying to frighten them, I'd be thinking they'd be trying to frighten me, but I knew about it anyhow, I'd be up shaving, and the room'd be, like as if somebody drew their fingers along the bars of the bed, there'd be nobody. It could be broad daylight you know.

PAULINE: *What was it?*

I don't know. We didn't take any notice eventually.

PAULINE: *– and May told me that you'd hear the latch of the door and the door opening –*

There were stories about it, that it was a Persse that owned that, not the Persse from Roxborough now, he was down in Moyode, there were two Persses, Roxborough Persse and Moyode Persse, 'twas a Moyode Persse that owned the land where my father's house was…but then, previous to that, I think the first one that was in it that I heard of anyhow, was a fellow by the name of Fairclough, a black Protestant. There was always a story anyhow that, that time they'd sow winter wheat, they'd sow it before the Christmas, they could sow it up to the end of January, but he wanted them to sow the wheat anyhow, Christmas Day, they said no, that it was a church holiday, so he let them off anyhow. Then it came to St Patrick's Day, that's the time you'd be sowing the oats, around Patrick's Day, he wanted them to sow the oats, they said no, it was the church holiday again. He said he wasn't having it anymore, he said, ye sow it. So they sowed it, it grew up a lovely crop, no head ever came on it. That's the story anyhow. But he was supposed to have died anyhow, a horse hearse came, and pulled up at the front gate, did you see the house, well there's a gate there, there was anyway, I don't know is it there yet. That's where the hearse pulled up. They brought out the coffin, put it into the hearse, the hearse driver got up and told the horses, 'go on, in the name of God'. They wouldn't stir. He told them three times anyhow, and a strange man walked out of the crowd, and he said, 'I'll drive them for you'. He got up and he called, 'Go on' and they went mad up the gate and into the bushes and were never seen again.

JOHN JONES

16 December 2003

I was born here in Cregclare. In this house. Eleven in
family, there was four sisters in England, two brothers,
three brothers in England – you have to think – and
that's my sister there, Margaret, you know that, and
Christy, you know Christy. My parents' names were
Herbert and Nora Jones, Nora was Lynskey, Ballylara.
And they lived here all their life, this house must be a
couple of hundred years old at least. Because I'm here
seventy years and my father was in it before me. He
was born here, and his father was here ... Do you

know where the big house was in Cregclare, where the Roches were? And another one here where Joe Dolan lived. And the Persses that lived in Cregclare, from Roxborough. And the Trotters lived here below where Joe Dolan lives. But anyhow. Can I tell you about when we were going to school?

Well I went to school to Labane here above. And once April would come there'd be no shoes. No toilets in the school that time. Outside in a shed they were, one side for the girls the other for the boys. No boots on anyone, no shoe at all, once April would come till you'd come to October, November again. We didn't have too far to come, but they came down from Coxtown walking, the roads wouldn't be tarred that time, stones there'd be, kids used to come down walking, often their bare feet, the toes would be cutting them, they'd take no notice in the world. Teachers – Tommy O Meara was one, Mr Flatley, Mrs Fahy, up in Tulira, John Moylan below, they were the four now.

PAULINE: *Once you'd leave school you'd come home, is that it?*

There was no such thing as anything else, Pauline. No, no, you came home and you'd go off around working for – I worked for Mattie Gilligan, that was the first, up in Raheen. I worked for Pat Reilly then, another neighbour. I worked with Eddie Bourke's for three years, I think, and I worked with Tomo Curtin for eighteen years, eighteen. I was very healthy always you know. You wouldn't feel the years going, sure. We used to have a bit of a lunch going to school, often we wouldn't have it at all, and we'd have to do without it. Your grandmother would know that too, so would your mother.

PAULINE: *What did you do as young lads to entertain yourselves?*

Round the woods sure. We'd go pulling nuts half the time. Hazel nuts. Pulling blackberries then and eating them, ah smathered, sure. And Saturday we'd be delighted with Saturday, you couldn't keep us down that time sure. I usen't do much dancing. We used to go up to the hall, looking in the windows, the priest after us 'Geddown' he'd say, he used to hunt us. Canon Considine. It was all bikes that time, rakes of bikes, no cars. Climbing up on top of the bikes. He couldn't hunt us off the road, you can't hunt anyone off the road. There's a place there beyond, it's a hole in the ground but there is a wall around it and that was where they used to say the Mass you know when, *Poll an Aifrinn.* There was another big hole, the Hangman's hole in Cregclare, they closed it there a few years ago, they should have left it, 'twas history like. Lord have mercy on your father, I'm sure you often heard him talk about the Hangman's hole, beyond the horseshoe. It was about fifty feet deep.

There was a house just opposite this, Hehirs, there was no gate, and for two hours or maybe three, hitting a ball up against the gables, no car. The doctor was the only car I met.

The furthest I went was Galway. I went to Croke Park a few times. I hurled, I was good all right but I never bothered with it much. We hadn't a hurl. And we played pitch and toss above in Labane every Sunday evening, on the road.

PAULINE: *Was life easier?*

Ah I don't think so. Might be happier. But you'd be working – twould be all – a pig then and he hanging out of the ceiling and a cut of piece of him down and put it in with the cabbage. I don't know but they were healthier [*days*], weren't they?

PAULINE: *Were you involved with the Moscows?*

No, no. They used to go across the country, no such thing as the road, and every wall, if 'twas every way high at all, down 'twould come. Give it the boot. They were up to John Kennedy's one night and they won a gramophone, put it on coming down, put it up on top of the pier and playing it at two o clock in the morning. The Canon had an awful set on them but they weren't that bad at all sure, only fooling.

PAULINE: *Was there much emigration in your time?*

There was, every second one was gone. Two sisters here, Eileen now she's the youngest, she's fifty years now, well she was gone and she wasn't sixteen at all. Fifty now. There's Betty, there's Mary, there's Eileen, there's Bridie, there's Herbert, Jimmy, in England. They went to London anyhow. Very hard on the parents, that's true.

We always used timber for the open fire. Ash is the best but it goes too quick, elm is the next but it is hard to light it, beech if you got beech there'd be nothing in Ireland to beat it, it would roast you. If the sap is in it, it won't light as well, but if you got it and dry it out a bit.

Foxes and badgers up in that wood. They'll be out there tonight.

MARY KATE LARKIN

3 October 2003

I was born in Killeeneen, my parents were Mick Forde
and Catherine Cahill. She was from Bruckagh, down
west, and he was from the village of Killeeneen. They
got married in 1918, 1919 – 1918, Seán was born in 1919

and I was born in 1920. But that was the way it was long ago. A child was born every year. There were seven of us, five girls and two boys.

The two boys are dead now, all the girls are alive, all in the 80s. I went to school in Killeeneen. It's gone now. 'Twas a pity all those schools and old houses were knocked down that time because they were very historical, I mean, the Walshes that lived there in Killeeneen, they had a lovely little cottage there, and Liam Mellows used be there, at that time, you know all those, all knocked, all gone now. We walked to school, then Seán and Seamus and I stayed at home because there was no jobs or anything that time, and then the other four went to secondary school, cycled, and Lily went to Loughrea to the convent there, we were getting a bit better off by that time. Five of us girls, four of them entered [*the convent*]. Three in Australia now. I was the only one that got married to keep the [*laughs*] breed going!

PAULINE: *And you had no interest in joining the nuns?*

No I hadn't. Ah we were put out working there, working the land. We had no social life until we came up to 18, 19, there was an old hall there in Kileeneen and there used be dances there and there was no dances any other where at the time. No. They used come from far and near, cycling. No such thing as a motor car. Two or three lads there playing the fiddle, the melodeon, dancing till 5 o'clock in the morning and the dust driven out of the floor. Oh 'twas great, 'twas great. We thought 'twas great anyhow. There was no drink, no drugs, a crowd of lads used come into our house every night, gambling, there'd be cardplaying there, and stories, we used to enjoy it. Nobody used go to the pub that time of course. If they went to a fair now, fairs there used be that time, if they went to a fair they'd have a couple of pints, bottles of stout.

Nowadays people don't meet each other. That time now I remember the men they'd be going to the fields and they'd meet each other and have a big long chat, now they meet on the road, it's two motor cars flying past, they barely salute each other. People don't know their own cousins.

PAULINE: *When did you meet your husband then?*

Sometime in 1945 or '6, at the hall in Craughwell. He asked me to dance, and that was it. Bicycles we had that time. He cycled me home. And back again. Men cycled miles dropping women home. Honest to God they were great. We met every Sunday night then, and that was it.

PAULINE: *Did you get engaged?*

No, no there was no engagement at all, we got married in 1947. We went into Galway, Jack had a cousin in Galway, she used be doing meals and things. But there was only father and mother and a few others. We hired a car. For the honeymoon, we went to Limerick for two nights, that was it. We went down on the bus to Limerick, and back on the bus again. I was delighted with it … When I moved in, his father was there. Jack's mother died when the youngest of the family was born, and there was six of them in it. So he had to rear them on his own. Oh he was great, he was a great worker, and he was great for minding the kids when I had to go out working with Jack. That was the way it was with everyone.

I had five children, two lads, three girls, Michael, Martin, Geraldine and Kathleen and Pauline. Geraldine entered the convent.

My sisters who entered, three of them entered down in Ballinamore in Mayo and they went from that to Australia and they're there ever since. They're – one of them's 80 now, the other one's 78 the other one's 76. They are in the one convent, they went nursing, a nursing order there; two of them were nursing and the other one is a chemist. They're not working or anything now, sure they killed themselves working, there was an awful lot of nuns that time went out after the war and they had no means or no way for doing anything, they had to do everything themselves. What year did they go, 1943 I think they went first, she didn't come home then, my father was dead then when she came home, my mother was alive all right, father was dead 19 years when she came. They were supposed never to come home when they went but then they said they'd give them time to come home every 15 years, but it was 19 years by the time her turn for coming home came. When they went, now, 'twas awful cruel, my parents never to see them again. My father never saw them again. Three years ago they came home last.

PAULINE: *What do you think is the biggest change in the last 70 years?*

Oh I don't know, it's all different sure. But once television came in, that finished it. There was no such thing as people going to visit, that time they'd come in at night to visit there and you'd get all the history there of long ago. Oh they were great that time. Compared with now. But I suppose when we were young that time we thought 'twas great but we're old now and see the young crowd coming up and what they have – I wouldn't wish for that on anyone. Because when they come up to 15 or 16 that's it. They won't take any heed of their parents or anyone. We did everything we were told long ago. Up till we were nearly 20. But now they're 15 and 16 they're all gone out to the bars.

The young crowd now they don't know anything else, you see. They don't know how we lived, and then the people don't tell them, they won't pretend to the young people now that they were as poor as they were, or the life they lived at all. There was 12 in families at home, now, and there was two bedrooms and a sitting room and a kitchen, and that was all. And there'd be 5 or 6 I suppose in every bed. There had to be you know. And no-one took one bit of notice.

18 September 2003

PAULINE: *Where are you from, Laurence?*

Dublin, Glasnevin.

PAULINE: *Were there many in your family?*

Four boys and four girls. My father was from Dublin and my mother was from Leitrim.

PAULINE: *Where did they meet, were you ever told?*

I have no idea, there was not, ah, discussion of the relationship between parents to children. But that would have been I think very characteristic of that era, it was the time when children were supposed to be seen and not heard, and the amount of communication between parents and children, and in my experience and I think it's wider than my experience, much less than today. Certainly in my case, and I know other people of my age it was the same. I think it is, you know every age has its own faults, its own weaknesses, and that would have been one of that period's weaknesses. It wasn't at all – you know I hate using terms like child-friendly, I hate using words like bonding, that sort of language, it borders on pop psychology, but I think every age does have its own deficiencies and its own downsides, I mean the present time, you take children being sent out to creches, etc, I disapprove of that entirely, but then that would be partially my own background, this may be old-fashioned, I believe the mother should be in the home until the children have reached at least primary school. I'm not saying the father can't do it as well. My earliest memories, I have no memories before the age of four, none at all, so it is as if I emerged out of the fog, fully formed, aged four.

PAULINE: *Where did you come in your family?*

Second.

PAULINE: *You had second-child syndrome had you?*

I imagine that has persisted, the second-child syndrome has persisted, but certainly the distance between, the lack of communication between parents and children was, in my opinion, extraordinarily severe. And I think it was partially fostered by, eh, when I was in the 1930s and 40s, by and large the Irish people, including my own people, would have been uneducated, and there's no tradition in my family of education, higher education, and all the people were either small farmers, or artisans, my father's people were brushmakers, in a factory in deathly places like Sheriff St. I would go down there on occasion with my uncle Peter, who was my, I have two or three favourite people, we'd go down the brush factory, it was in a loft, it was Dickensian, and there'd be all these gnarled old men with gnarled old hands sitting around a big cauldron of tar – making sweeping brushes – and they would do this at remarkable speed, but they all seemed to me to be old men, they all seemed to be small, they all seemed to be hunchbacked, that was real Dickensian-type industry, it was almost pre-industrial, I mean it would have been one of the early stages of industrialization. You'd see them all sitting around, about half a dozen, and they'd be chatting away, and they'd be singing, and they seemed to be as happy as larry. But then in those days people didn't have any expectations, above and beyond coming along and making their brushes and getting their pittance at the end, of the week, which would have been enough to put food on the table but not a very rich or varied diet, you know, and they would have lived in artisan dwellings, corporation-type dwellings and so on. It was generally believed, then, [*laughs*] there was a general belief that the higher-up people in society carried the greatest level of stress, but research has proven, apparently, the reverse, that the higher-up you are the less stress you have, and that it's the poor – I must say I found from the time I worked to the time I retired, I mean, I went up in the hierarchy, and I would have been one of these people who would have been believed to carry stress, and my colleagues and my superiors would have been partners etc – they didn't carry any stress at all! They had a ball! They used to go to finance meetings where all the top brass would sit, and another man and myself, I was an engineer, we were the two executives to the committee, and these weighty men to whom we submitted our proposals – they had it made, they were just pedalling their way towards retirement, they couldn't care less. Some funny things used to arise from it, I used to take it seriously [*laughs*]. I did suffer a certain amount of stress, because we were expected to answer for the amount of expenditure, millions and millions. So any time I had to submit something, which I felt there was issues in it beyond my competence, I would write a little note beside my plan, my plan would be contingent on certain decisions made, xyz and my chief used to laugh and refer to 'Bob's position papers'. You got the impression that position papers were not popular.

PAULINE: *Now we'll go back. Where did you go to National school?*

The first school I went to was a school in North Great George's St run by the nuns, I was only there a very short while. And in fact it was in the nuns' school in North Great Georges St that I had my first ever punishment. And I'm afraid that it was rather embarrassing. One day at school, it might have been the very first day, through nerves or what have you, I made a mess of myself in school. And I remember being taken home and being chastised, and abused, I remember being humiliated, it was a traumatic experience, the first experience of life I had, no experience like it before that. But I remember that as being so – humiliating. They made me feel humiliated. I was only there a very short while and then I went to an all-Irish-speaking primary school in Marlborough St. I must say my experience of school, certainly up to the time I was 13, was horrible. My experience of school was constant trauma. When I went to this primary school there were maybe a dozen small kids who were entering school for the first time. And on our first day there we were put into a certain room while they were waiting to see what they'd do with us, and in this room there were desks, and all the little boys, we were all on our best behaviour except me. And I took great pleasure in lifting the lid of the desk and banging it down, it made a tremendous racket. And after this went on once or twice, some giant opened the door – he was about ten feet tall – and he came in and he beat the living daylights out of me. That was my second experience of school.And my experience of school until I left the Christian Brothers and went to the Dominicans was constant, constant beating. Never stopped. I went to – after Marlborough St for a couple of years – I then went to Coláiste Mhuire. Which was famous for its nationalism. For its Gaelgeorism. For its fascism. I remember on one occasion one brother giving a lecture in praise of Nazi Germany. It's hard to believe! [*laughs*] There were people in Ireland at that stage whose hatred of England was such – now I'm not saying it was widespread but there were little pockets of it – and I remember a Christian Brother giving a lecture to this effect. When I went to Colaiste Mhuire I already had traumatic experiences, I was afraid, I was terrified going to school, and in all the years I was in Colaiste Mhuire I used to get thrashed, every day, non-stop. And it's a funny sort of thing if you get into the habit of being thrashed, you expect to be thrashed, and your expectations are never disappointed. Now I wasn't the only one being thrashed. But in this school, it was a fiercely Gaelgeoir sort of school, my father happened to leave Ireland, and join the RAF. And it was known in the school that our father was in the RAF fighting for the King, and with a name like Laurence, I mean I remember very clearly if that was the situation, if you had a name like Laurence or a name like Smith, or any non-Irish name, you were collectively grouped together, but if you had a name like Oisin O Siochrú or Cian McGinley or something like that, you were up the front. I know people will say that that isn't true, but that's my recollection of it. And I'm certain – though my recollection could be modified

– I'm certain there was a very distinct element of that there. But I went to school – every day I went to school up to the age of 13 with fear and dread every day, I used get thrashed everyday. And a certain number of us used to. But so much so – and you couldn't tell your parents. If you told your parents it would be 'Well, you deserve it' – and you have incidentally, just looking forward, all this stuff comes out on the television and you get the fellows who say, 'Ah sure it didn't do me a bit of harm'. I believe that that is totally false, and I believe that the generation produced by that system, which that system produced, is nervous, cautious, people lacking self-esteem, lacking ambition.

PAULINE: *It had to leave a scar –*

Oh it did, oh absolutely. And I'm quite convinced that a very large number of students who went to certain schools in particular, some schools had a reputation for it, you know, I mean, like Artane, which wasn't a school as such, but. There were places which had a reputation for this. Other places didn't, other Christian Brothers' schools didn't, it seemed to depend very much – even though they were all Christian Brothers, some schools seemed to have an ethos of its own, maybe derived from the original head of that school, etcetera, maybe the brothers they took on, as brothers. That's my experience of school, constant beating. And I used to share last and second-last place in every subject, with a poor eejit called XY. And he really was thick. Poor fellow. He really was thick. And he and I used to be thrashed every day. My recollection of it is walking up Parnell Square up into that school in a state of dread. And I remember on one occasion we had a science class, funny the little things you remember, the details you remember, yet vast areas you can't remember detail at all. But we used to have a science class every

Saturday morning, and you had to submit your lab reports. And every Saturday morning he would hand back these reports. And for those whose reports were not good enough he would say, *'Amach libh'* – out into the line. And myself and XY used to be in the line every Saturday of our lives, and we used get thrashed, every Saturday. And the thrashing, it actually was vicious. It wasn't getting slapped, no you were in agony, and of course there was a requirement that you didn't cry. Anyway one day as I got older, I said to myself, 'This doesn't seem reasonable, that I'll get thrashed every Saturday'. So I decided to put it to a test. So one day I got my notebook and I ensured that it was perfect in every sense of the word, handwriting, oh everything great, the content was great, made a special effort, and got the assistance of others etcetera to ensure that it was absolutely A–1. Saturday morning, *'Labhras amach'* I was thrashed. So when things like that happen, you abandon hope, you know. Mind you they always left you with a sense of guilt that it is your fault, that you're a bad boy, but on the other hand I also had some objective knowledge, that I – Fortunately my mother decided to take myself and my older brother and send us to Newbridge to boarding-school when I was 13.

PAULINE: *And was your other brother getting thrashed as well?*

Not as much as me. I think there's a certain look on a person's face that invites thrashing. Impertinent, or something. Jim used to try and bribe the teachers. I remember he told me on one occasion he offered one of the teachers a penny if he wouldn't beat him. I think my mother was actually getting the message at this stage, that the whole scene was really appalling. So she sent myself and Jim to Newbridge. The thing about this is that, on the start of the next term, the first term of the next year, my two younger brothers who were still in Colaiste Mhuire, were sent home with a note stating that if Colaiste Mhuire is not good enough for the older boys it's not good enough for the younger boys. And they were expelled. So mother who was a real tough cookie – my mother was as tough as nails, I think she overdid the toughness then but she was as tough, as shrewd, as worldly-wise, in terms of worldly-wise she reared four idiot sons, you know what I mean, not one of us has her toughness or her shrewdness. I mean, I can be shrewd for five minutes but real shrewdness means, all the time. Well anyway she went up to the brothers and they refused to see her, then she wrote to the principal, or the Provincial whatever they called him, no reply, wrote to various people no reply, wrote to the bishop, no reply, but then she got my two younger brothers into another Christian Brothers school, St Vincents, Glasnevin, and they were in there, and after one day they were sent home, they were expelled from there. And then she got them into some other Christian Brothers school, and after one day they were – there was a conspiracy, a clearcut conspiracy, that these boys were not to be allowed into any Christian Brothers school. Which was discrimination of a very serious nature, because in those days the vast majority of schools were run by the Christian Brothers, I mean, there were a few private schools, so Mother as I say, was a tough woman, so she went to her solicitor, and the solicitor said the usual etcetera, she got no satisfaction, so she took them to court. Which was a very brave thing to do in those days, when the Church could do no wrong and believe me in those days the Church could not do wrong, in fact if you raised your hand against the church, raised your voice against the church, they had ways of ostracising you, you know they would make it clear to everybody that these people are not good people.

PAULINE: *Noel Browne stood up, didn't he, to the Church?*

Oh yes, I was there the day that the day that the canon told the young girls of the parish to have nothing to do with this communist. But anyway she took them to court, oh no response from them at all, till eventually the court case came along, and of course they still didn't turn up, their barrister turned up and made a settlement out of court. And they had to make a very generous settlement because Mother would not make a soft settlement. She got a very substantial settlement, which, she gave some to charity, some was used for their subsequent education and some went I believe into Mother's General Exchequer you know *[Laughs]* …

When I went to Newbridge there was biffing but it was actually harmless, you got so many stars in the day from teachers and you went along to the biffing room, and the poor old biffer was hated, and you could bargain against the number of points you had, it was a joke. It wasn't completely a joke, you know, they had to give it some sort of cred. So when I was in Newbridge I was on the only Newbridge team that ever won the Leinster Rugby Cup, I was Captain of the school in my last year, and I showed first or second place in every subject. Education became dead easy to me,

PAULINE: *But you were the lucky one, how many kids didn't have – and were destroyed –*

Absolutely, absolutely. And when you hear this business about abuse in the industrial schools, I'm sure the abuse there was greater, because they were totally in control, but there was a huge amount of abuse went on in the ordinary schools too. By the same token I don't mean to be tarring every one with the same brush, there was some places where there was pockets of it, probably in the industrial schools too, individuals, all it needs are individuals to make the ethos, or they would hire in – and they would get away with it because there was a belief, a very definite belief, that the cane – 'spare the rod and spoil the child' There was a very definite belief that physical punishment was the only way to rear children.

IN LOVING MEMORY

— of —

Eamonn Linnane
Tullira,
Ardrahan, Co. Galway
who died
on the 28th May 2004
Rest in Peace

2 December 2003

Eamonn was born in Tulira in the castle grounds and lived there until he was 9 or 10. His father Owen worked there; he got this house built. Eamonn stayed at school until he was 14. He got a job in Tulira doing post in the evenings, posting letters and so on.

I worked for old Lord Hemphill, Lady Hemphill divorced him and came back again. She is buried above in Kilmacduagh.

Then I turned around at 16 or 18 lived above there in the castle for 3 years, never saw a thing only a blind bat. Paid a shilling a week.

There used to be around 20 or 25 of us gathered out there, nowhere to go and no money, tricking and dancing out there at the cross, no motor cars that time. There were the Nilands, Divineys, Cunninghams, Murrays, Whelans and ourselves and off to a game of cards, any wall that was a bit too high, we weren't shy, we knocked them.

Out of going to Gort I met her ladyship, I had cattle at the fair, she came over looking at the cattle, it was over looking at me she was, and out of that we made a little date. If I was caught around Crow Lane I would have been hung. Out of that we got married, 50 years married next month, we went off to Dublin on our honeymoon I had a couple of cattle and I sold one; I suppose Rose had a few pounds. I stayed working all my life in Tulira. Lord and Lady Ann came about 50 years, when they came first, they used invite all the parishioners in for Christmas, that all stopped. I did every kind of work for £6 10s a week.

For entertainment we used to go to the pictures in Gort or if the marquee was anywhere around Gort, Labane, Craughwell, whole gangs of us would cycle down. I remember Jim Quinn, D Murray we would go into Gort for a few drinks we would have no money but we would make up half a crown to go into the dance in Labane, one would go in the others would go through the window the priest [*Canon Considine*] got wise to that and painted the window sill green the night before and we got stuck to it.

I was part of the 'Moscow' crowd we had great fun altogether. One night a gang of us decided we would go for apples, there was a pit below at Miko Barretts, we went into the garden it was all clay, we rooted out as much apples as we could. I am sure he went stone cracked in the morning.

Hurling then, in the priest's field there would be 100 down there, they were good times. There is a lot dead now, there is only 4 or 5 of us alive now, Tomo Mc went awful quick Colie Geoghegan, Ned Quinn, Lowry Murray, they are all gone – Mike Fada, Milo Mullins. There were 6 in my family they are all gone to Heaven, except myself. Jack, Oliver, Arthur, Vincent and Maureen.

FRANK McHUGH

31 January 2004

I was born in Co. Sligo, Monasteraden, Co. Sligo. It's in county Sligo and it's about four mile from Ballaghadereen and about four mile from Gurteen. Ballaghadereen is in Roscommon and Gurteen is in Sligo. There were eight children. Five boys and three girls. Our school was half a mile from where I was born. And I was born in 1919.

I left National school at 12, and I had a couple of years then in St Nathy's College, Ballaghadereen.

There wasn't much for anybody that time, and I left that then, and I went to England about 16 or 17 year old. I started off as a pageboy in a hotel. Working the lift and answering the door and so on and so forth.

PAULINE: *That was a nice enough job wasn't it?*

Ah 'twas not. I could easily have got as good a job at home in Ireland but the wages that time were simply chronic. Ten shillings a week now I was paid for that job in England and tips, about 1935, '36. I wanted to stay in England but I was back and forth to England for a number of years, and I was in England for a lot of the war, London, and during the war I was at Berkshire, building airports, concrete, laying runways and so forth. I used to come back and forth to England from home, myself and my next-door neighbour we used to do a lot of contract work, cutting turf and mowing meadows, cutting turf with a sleane and mowing the meadow with a scythe, and we didn't think anything, we had no problem with it, we worked away, during the periods that I would be home, and go back to England whenever things were slack here.

PAULINE: *So you were one of 'the men who built Britain'?*

Well, same as anyone during the war years. I was staying in London with my sister for a good bit of the war, she was there – I was there for air raids, and I was there when the doodlebugs came over. They were a pilotless bomb and we heard them coming and my brother who was well-used to the armaments said, 'That's not a plane now, that's something new'. Then there'd be silence and you could start counting then, ten, fifteen, twenty, I forget what it was, and you'd hear a big bang. Once the engine stopped the arc swung in eight seconds, it would come down and explode, it was Hitler's latest invention. They were terrorizing the English, people were used to terrible things by that time, so they didn't worry about it. But eventually the British army got a way of beating them and they intercepted them before they got into London. Most women and children were evacuated from London at that time. They went down the country, including, at one period my sister came over to live in Ireland, but it didn't suit her, she went back again. It was a really, really tough time, no doubt about it.

Then my father got sick in 19 – he was sick beforehand, but he got really sick in about 1943, '44, '43 and I came home and stayed for a period. He improved, I went away again for a while, but a friend of mine wrote to me that he wasn't too well again, so I came home again and stayed until he died, in 1945. And I didn't go back again then except on a holiday to see where I was. I did, I stayed in the home place then for a year, and the year 45–6, and I bought a school residence in an adjoining village, so I rented that and set up a shop and carried on from there until 1947, we had tremendous snow, and we had snow that time until May, from January, yes it was six to eight feet high in places, the roads, you couldn't see them, and to clear the main roads with whatever machinery they had at that time. We at that time didn't have a delivery for ten weeks, during 1947, and before that period I started building a little shop for myself, and I was held up with that till May Day, and I got it finished at the end of May, and got married in 1948. To Bridie.

Bridie was working for my uncle down in Monasteraden, in his business place, and we met there, and we were going out for a long time. She was from Geevan, the other end of Sligo, but she was a very conscientious worker, a wonderful type, there's no doubt about it.

Well, we were in that shop that I built, and in 1952, a pub came up for sale four miles away from where we had a shop. And I said to Bridie, should we try and buy it. We had a little collateral from business so on and so forth. So we kept it quiet, and it was for sale for a long time, and eventually we bought that pub. So we left our grocery shop then, we sold it, and took over this pub, then, and we done a bit of work on that, cleaned it up, and in nine, ten months time the man that sold it, the last man that owned it, wanted to buy it back from me. So I went one day to town anyway to buy some cabbage plants [*laughs*] and lo and behold I met him and so on and so forth, we had a chat, and he made me an offer for the pub I bought, which I couldn't refuse. So he took it over then. Myself and Bridie saw the ad for this pub, at least 'twas Bridie that saw it, 'twas classed as Taylor's Hotel that time. I came into the auction, before I came to the auction and I came up and had a look and so on and so forth, and we took it over after the Galway Races 1954. We're here since. That was a pub now that usen't be open on a Sunday, and used close very early every other evening, so we changed and put in a new counter so on and so forth, and we enjoyed every minute we were in it. And Bridie, every day, she was very glad.

PAULINE: *And how much was the pub when you bought it that time?*

And that time it was an awful price, we thought. It was four or five thousand pounds. At that time it was a lot of money. So I probably wouldn't have been able to buy it only for selling the pub at a profit. But all property was cheap that time. Oh I loved Ardrahan. No problem at all with it. We spent a lot of time painting. And Bridie loved it, yes. And Patricia was born. Frances was a few months old when she landed, and Patricia was born when we were so-many years here. Yeah, we enjoyed it, we had no problems. Wonderful crowd of customers. And I don't think we ever had any serious problem at all. It was classed I'd say more as a rambling house than a – well you see the money wasn't in it that time for heavy drinking. If it was, I don't know what would happen, but the money wasn't in it, and people were depending on the beet and the cattle and the corn and nearly all them things – the corn and the beet is gone now. But a fair day, that was the one day you could always be ready to go to the bank and lodge the takings and get you out of trouble for the next few months. Doing all these buyings now, you had arrangements made for an overdraft, and you had to keep – the banks were pretty strict, you had to keep within your limits. I suppose the same thing happens today. Thanks be to God I don't have much dealings with it. We had a little grocery shop at the end of the pub. We cordoned that off, because it was a law that came in that time, that groceries had to be separated from a bar, and of course it made sense too. And we installed air extractors, and that's a long long time.

My mother died in 1922, November 1922, when my brother was born, so our business broke up then after that, and my father went to live down the road with his father and mother and look after the land. And four of us – there was eight of us in it – were taken to America by aunts, and four left at home. And the four of us then grew up together.

It was sad, and in the case of one, Ann, who joined the nuns, the Sisters of Charity, or, can't think of the name, who I'm going out to see one of the days, I hope, in Boston, she joined the convent, and what I was going to say, the first time I ever saw her after she left home was [*becomes very moved*] in Ardrahan, after we were in it for a long time. I was in Ardrahan and I owned the place and she was only released after Pope John XXIII made new rules that allowed them [*the nuns*] out. And that was the first time I met Ann. Now I had met my brother Tom during the war, he was a soldier in Northern Ireland, and Larry came home, a couple of times, Mamie, the other sister, came home but got drowned on Lecarrow down at Sligo, she was about 27 or 28, she had come home from America.

The four of us that stayed at home, John the youngest went to America and he joined the American army, and finished up as Lieutenant-General, and died in 1969, I was over at his funeral. P.J. stayed in England, got married, settled down, and after so many years went to Canada, and his wife and family, P.J. is dead now, and so is John, and their wives are dead, but we're in contact with their families all the time. Betty got married in London, and went to Australia, with her family and she had children and great-grandchildren which come fairly regular to us now, we had one at Christmas, she has come back three or four times, she is only two years younger than me, I was talking to her only last night, and she was all excited about us going to see Annie. And her first question was, will ye come and see me next? [*laughs*].

I have no regrets over one bit of it, not one bit, only when I think of the past and the present, I see that there's no comparison in lifestyle. And even though everything is modernised now, I still think that we enjoyed ourselves to the full, and had a lot less – enjoyed going out trying to catch rabbits. There was no such thing that time as going to the pubs. I remember the older people, my aunts and the senior people, there was only two or three times in the year that they'd go, except if they were going to a fair, they might have a couple of drinks on a fair day, but otherwise there was no such thing.

Tom McCarron

16 March 2004

I'm from a place called Kinawley, Co. Fermanagh, on the borders of Cavan. There were five in my family. I emigrated in 1958 to London and spent 32 years there. Most of the time I was a bus-driver, for 30 years. I worked at all kinds of jobs, menial jobs [*laughs*], my sister is in California, another sister died ten years ago, a brother who lives in London and another brother who lives in London. They're all gone from home and emigrated fairly young, it's a funny thing we didn't really – in the '50s people were emigrating and we were lucky enough not to be forced to emigrate, my father was well-off, but people were coming back on holidays showing off and saying how lovely it was over there, and when you went over there it wasn't like that at all [*laughs*] you were so proud, you had to fight to go, then you wouldn't give in, when it wasn't like you thought it was.

PAULINE: *And how were you treated in England being from the north of Ireland?*

Well I honestly – I never came up against any prejudice and I sometimes think you can avoid all that if you behave yourself. If you misbehave yourself you'll get prejudice, but I always felt the average Englishman was first-class, gave me no bother at all. The only time I ever came across, working in the public as a bus-driver, the only time I ever got any trouble was from the Irish people, coming out of pubs, dancehalls things like that. But the average Englishman never gave me any trouble, any trouble. This was long before there was any Asians or West Indians or Africans, with nobody coming only Irish. And I always say that, any time – I spent thirty-odd years, lived in fairly bad conditions, I met Eileen – Eileen was only 19 when we got married and I was just gone 20, and we had four kids then – we had three kids in three years [*laughs*] and another one two years later, and we lived in very bad conditions, we did all right in later years. I was lucky. But eh – then there was other people that had worse flats than we had, and when I go back on holidays and I see people that I'd have known years and years ago, and some of them had a really bad time, living rough, and I was lucky enough I got a job that paid a pension, things like that, as a bus-driver. It was not big money but it was steady, and there was a pension, but there was a lot of those things [*i.e. building work*] in the '50s and '60s, there was much more money and they didn't pay any tax, but then when it come to age 50, nobody wanted them and there was no security, it is rather sad actually. But then they had it good when I had it bad, so?

We had our share of illnesses as well you know. Eileen got ill, he sent her to a TB hospital. Now I'm talking about the early 60s, nobody went there except people that were really bad … so he sent her there, and I don't think it went down too well with my family, so we were talking about that in the last few days, because she said even the doctors and the nurses the TB was finished at the time, it was on an island as well, and there was no transport, and I only got to see her twice, and she didn't know anyone, there were old girls, she was 21, weren't you [*to Eileen*]? And everyone was over 60 and she was the only young person in there, and there was an old girl of 60 said to her, 'you'll be back' and this was awful depressing now.

PAULINE: *Why did you come to Galway? Why didn't you go back up to Fermanagh?*

Oh well we got what you call an Irish paper in London called the *Irish Post*, It's still going, started in the late 50s. And we used look up the advertisments, advertising houses all over Ireland, and we just happened to see this one in Galway, we were looking at a place in Edgeworthstown. That's the one we thought we were going to get. And Labane just come up and even the lady that we bought the house from, she said it was sold, and then we wrote to it again, the people who were buying it couldn't come up with the money or something, it fell through, still the market …

EILEEN: But Galway was the place we wanted to come to, six miles from where my father was born –

TOM: you know Killina – that's where her ancestors come from –

PAULINE: *And would you not like to have gone back to the north –*

No it never appealed to me. I like going up there and I never really liked it, because [*laughs*] I had a pub, on the borders, I owned a pub when I was 17, well my father owned it he was going to give it to me, and these people were always coming in and fighting about religion and on a fair day they 'd be coming in arguing there was always animosity, long before the Troubles, you know, and I never liked it, I certainly wouldn't go and live there. I like to visit. My father had a shop. And he was pretty well-off. And this was during the war, now when I would be a kid. Mid-forties. And most people didn't have any food, but we weren't short because we had – there was ration books but you always got enough because you were in the shop. Talking about sweets and chocolate and things that most people didn't get so I'd gave a little bit to them, you know. So there was a little bit of prejudice, and I got a bit bullied for that, other kids, maybe some of them nine or ten kids living in really bad conditions, I used to have to steal sweets to give them. And then I started – actually we were talking about this the other day – I was the first one in Co. Fermanagh, certainly the first outside Enniskillen, my father was brought to court for [*my*] not going to school. And in those days that was rare, most kids would be from a farming background and allowed to have a lot of time off making hay, turf or whatever. But I lived right beside the school, so there was no excuse for it. I wouldn't go to school. Truancy. I'd climb trees, and on one occasion I remember going down fishing about a mile or two away from where I lived, and bad luck was on my side that day who was fishing over the other side only the priest, and he never said a word to me the next morning.

But I remember, I can't remember what age I was, but there was this teacher, our regular teacher, she was good, the basics when I left, reading and writing, she was having a baby every year, and there was always a stand-in teacher when she was having time off, and most of them would be somebody, well, one or two might be qualified teachers but most of them weren't, and most of them were all right but this particular one, I'll always remember her, and she didn't like me or she didn't like the family, but she had a system which was absolutely – nobody had ever heard of it before, But whoever got the most slaps of the cane, got an extra six, and those who got the least got a bar of chocolate. And I qualified for the extra six. I would have been about nine or ten. I'll skip a bit. Then my father – he was very old-fashioned, he made a lot of money, I'll tell you how rich he had become, he bought a castle, with 175 acres, some of it was in the south, some in the north, then he bought lots of other property. And he didn't get married till late in life, so he thought it would be a good thing to bring his family to do the same as what he done, so he sent me off to a place seventeen miles outside Belfast, an hotel, to work as a barman, or whatever, and it was one of the posh places, and it had swing doors, and I never heard tell of swing doors, and my brother that left me down, the one we went to see in the north, he had a part to play in it as well, because he worked there, and then when he left there – he thought it was great because he had a great time there – my father bought him a pub, then he run off with some girlfriend to London – but when I arrived at this place anyway, this lady called Mrs Wilkins, it was really posh, I had to call the daughter 'Miss Norma' and the son 'Master Bobby'. And when my brother left me there, he drove off in a van with somebody, and this lady, with the glasses hanging down here, she said 'come into the office', and she interviewed me in the office. 'How old are you now?', 'fifteen' and she said, 'you shouldn't be here'. I went there for £3 a week now. 'I can't employ you, you're underage, all I can do is £1 a week gratuity and your meals, tips, no wages'. So he was gone, I'm 100 miles away from home, no money, no phones, and do you know I spent six months, and I never went outside the door, and it was one of those awful places, full of prejudice, and don't tell them what part you are from, and I didn't know but I was there, three months at the latest, two months, but I had no money to get home, and I had a bit of pride, and somebody told me how to get to where I could thumb a lift home. I don't remember how I got home, but the sad thing of it was, when I got home, my parents said to me, it must have been the afternoon or the evening, 'go up to the pub', my brother had done a bunk. Without as much as saying hello or how are you [*laughs*]. And that is a fact. They were the worst two years of my life in that pub. I was 16 when I took over the pub. And they were all fighting. This was a busy pub now. We go in there when we go on holidays and it still is a busy pub. I didn't live there, I lived four miles away and I used to sometimes have to walk home, I couldn't drive or nothing, and I used to walk and I was afraid of ghosts and I was afraid of B-Specials and I used to whistle and I made sure I wasn't going to whistle a rebel song [*laughs*]. I remember on one occasion this fellow who I knew, stopped me. And he said, 'what's your name Thomas'. You know he stopped me there, 'what's your name Thomas', so I said my name and he knew well what my name was, you know, they were all from around the area, all locals, all Protestants in those days, but I spent two years there. Then the troubles, the 1950s troubles broke out, I don't know if you ever heard of the border campaign, around south Fermanagh, the IRA started blowing up bridges and things like that, and then anybody that was around my age, 17 or 18, if anything happened they would pull you in, and I suppose they'd question and interrogate you, and I suppose in those days they'd ask you to sign the oath of allegiance to the Queen. And if you were an IRA man you wouldn't sign the oath and you'd be interned. But I signed the oath of allegiance four times, I kissed her arse if you like! [*laughs*]. But I remember what really started it up, there was a fellow, he come into the pub around midnight, and two other fellows, and I didn't know this fellow. I knew one of the fellows that was with him, and they wanted to have a drink you know, and it was after closing time, they wanted to have one, a quick one, so I brought them into the kitchen in the bar, and then in the kitchen I had two fellows, two Protestants, one of them was a B-Special, looking for me. But anyways, I lived two sides of the border, but there was a mile in between customs' posts, the northern customs post and the southern customs post, and you couldn't drive across the border, in those days, you had what they called a bond that you had to get stamped to go over the border. And in those days the customs was closing before midnight, so there was no way you could cross the border, so these two fellows had a van the other side of the border, which was a mile. Seemingly these two fellows or three fellows went to cross the border. Now this Christmas both [*customs posts*] had been blown up umpteen times and there would have been plenty B-Specials undercover guarding it, you know what I mean. I never seen it but they said – but seemingly these two fellows who lived near the border were drunk, one of them was drunk anyway, so they went down, and they asked them to stop and they run off and one of them got shot, and I didn't know nothing about it, and I went home. Next morning, the Sunday morning, knock on the door and the police come and arrested me and brought me back to the station, interrogated me. I didn't have time to put my shoes on, they put me in a cell and I remember asking one of them who was there, a policeman, who I knew, and then the B-Special man was there, and the other fellow was there, and they said the same thing as I said, because I was telling the truth. And there was nothing going on. And the other side said that because I was with the B-Specials that I set them up, you know. So I couldn't win. Anyway they interrogated me, anyway I had nothing to do with anything like that. So anyway when I got released I went across the border, and I got arrested again. And the sergeant said to me, 'I know you didn't tell them nothing up there but you can tell me'. So I says – 'I don't know nothing!' [*laughs*]. Then I suppose I would have been 18 at that time, and then anything that ever happened there was always suspicion you know. But anyway, some time later, I went to Mass on a Sunday morning, might have been two or three months later, went to Mass and was walking up – because I lived beside the church and the school – the Orange Hall was right opposite the way, the police station right beside us, was walking up the aisle, I was always late for Mass, I was standing up for the first Gospel [*laughs*] and all the windows of the Church went in and all the panes, all blown up, somebody had blown up the Orange Hall, half-ten Mass. So when I got out, there was a policeman waiting, wanting to know who was last in [*big laugh*].

As usual I was always last in. Of course I was arrested with one or two other people, and brought down to Enniskillen and interrogated, and I told them the truth again. And they asked me all sorts of questions and I told them I didn't know, afterwards they let me out. But afterwards, it was getting to that extent that I said, 'I've got to go, I've get to get out of the country', you know, it was getting beyond – it wouldn't have got any better, but anyways, I emigrated to England in 1958, and I remember coming home on holidays six months later and they had this new Orange Hall … and I remember this old boy, he was the Master of the Orange Lodge, saw me crossing, and he said to me, 'Thanks very much for the new hall' [*big laugh*]. They got a new hall built! Because it was an old wreck of a hall, that was just the way he said it to me you know, so he was convinced that I'd done it, and everybody was convinced that I'd done it, but I had no knowledge, no knowledge at all of that. But anyway, I went then to London.

JOSIE McINERNEY

17 March 2004

I called to see Josie McInerney in Gort, originally from Ardrahan. I had planned to interview his brother Thomas (Tommo) who died … 'Lord have mercy on him'.

My grandfather was Michael McInerney from Cahermore Cross, Ardrahan, the family is no longer there now, his wife was McLoughlin, they had a number in family, they had a daughter who went to America before the census in 1901, relations of one of them called to me recently. There were four boys in the family, my father was one of them, his name was Tom, they lived at the crossroads there, they had a forge. My father got involved in the Republican Volunteer movement, he was imprisoned in 1916.

PAULINE: *Where was he imprisoned?*

He was in Frongach, he always told me it was a recruiting ground for volunteers, there was 60,000 of them in together, he got to know Michael Collins with whom he kept up correspondence until Michael Collins's death. He was a Commandant in the Volunteers. The house was burned by the Black and Tans, actually it was burned I believe the same night the hall in Labane was burned and John (Croppy) Joyce's house was burned – where Johnny Joyce is now. My father and Croppy Joyce camped out in the woods.

PAULINE: *How many were in your family?*

There were three boys Tommo, Miko and myself, no girls, I was the baby. I relied on Tommo a lot for advice on agriculture; if you asked him a question he wouldn't answer you in haste.

PAULINE: *Where did you go to school?*

We went to school in Labane, Tommo went to the Vocational School in Gort and I went to school in Gort. Miko went to St Mary's in Galway. Mike went to UCG then – Tommo or I didn't pursue education. I spent a few years in Gort and Tommo went to Agricultural School.

PAULINE: *What brought you to Gort?*

Well my father was a Rates Collector, he was appointed in 1922 – I was appointed in 1952 in the Gort district all around Gort, Kilbeacanty, Beagh and areas around. In 1957 I got married and lived in the Square in Gort and built a house here.

PAULINE: *How did you get into auctioneering?*

Well I started actually in 1962 – I was a rate collector up until 1985. I had an interest in it, if you have an interest you might succeed. The first house I did was the contents of the parochial house in Labane in 1962. Canon Considine had a huge amount of stuff collected while he was alive, that was the first house auction I did.

My school days in Labane. Mrs Fahy in the early years – one of the people that impressed me most in my whole life – Mr Slattery he was an absolutely wonderful man wonderful teacher – he put emphasis on different things, punctuality, truth and honesty.

PAULINE: *Did you play hurling?*

I used to play a bit I used to hurl for Ardrahan, Galway minors and played a few matches for Galway seniors, League matches – Miko that played – Tommo used hurl but not that much – we were interested in hurling.

PAULINE: *What was your mother's maiden name?*

She was Baker from Kilmacduagh. They got married in 1924, a beautiful gold medal was presented to them when they got married – he gave it to me before he died – from his comrades in the old IRA.

My father died in 1969, my mother died in 1985. She was younger than him – different characters – if she had something to tell you she would say it there and then, he would wait until the day after. He was living in Kellys' in Tulira, my memory of him is coming from Gort to Labane cycling, later years he had a car.

I took a lot of interest in exercise, not to be slouching around. My father told me Fr Considine could be relied on when my father was on the run from the Black and Tans – he had very strong republican views.

16 December 2003

May was born in the two-storey house down the road, and moved to Limepark when she was eleven. She said she 'was a bad mixer' because there was no house close to them.

She went to school in Peterswell. She moved to Limepark with her two brothers Jack and Paddy, she stayed there because it was closer to school, her first job was in Kiltulla for Lawlesses, they had a shop, she was paid a 'few bob a week'. She did some light housework to pay her fee.

She came home and spent a year 'knocking around Limepark'. She made Limepark her home. She went to Dublin against her family's will – 'they thought she would be corrupted'. She worked in a hotel for nine years until 1943. She met her husband there, the hotel was the Dublin Service flats, one half of the tenants were permanent residents, and a portion was kept for the Horse Show and theatre shows. This was a private place.

'I wanted to go to England to see the war'. So she got a reference and went to High Wykeham in Buckinghamshire. They stayed in a hostel. It was lovely, it had a reading room, dining room and recreation room and the best of food. When she got pregnant she had to go home, this was about one month before D-Day. Roger went to the Irish Consulate to get her out. She got out on compassionate grounds and she stayed in Dublin in a bed and breakfast in Westland Row.

They were burning turf for the train engines, no coal or oil that time – 'you would keep up to them on a bicycle'. There was no dining carriage that time, 'when we got to Athlone I got out for a drink of water. The train left without me', so she got home to Loughrea 'in a turf wagon'. She stayed at home and worked in Bradley's Pub for two years, Roger was still in England looking for some place to stay in titled houses to work.

They worked for Lady Kilmanty and stayed there for nine years, 'the daughter still writes to me.

When this land came up for sale we bidded on the lot, 107 acres. We went back to England to work for two more years to get more money to build a house. People around here were complaining that the Land Commission would take it off us. We started to build a shed and bought a range and a few bits and pieces. We lived in the shed for four years. It was just Hell in the beginning, it was the biggest mistake ever coming home'. They left England in 1954.

'The Black and Tans – I remember there was 2 soldiers shot up in Castledaly, the Howleys always went around with 2 threshing wheels.

Jack, Paddy and I were eating our dinner and shots passed over our heads. They used to bring Dad out occasionally and beat him. Uncle Mike, Willie and Pete out on the mountain, we never saw then, only they might come at night very late for a cup of tea.

A lot of them flocked above Peterswell. The three Howleys were in it, Mick escaped and ran fifteen miles across the heather, they had horse soldiers, he would lie on the heather and escaped.

Michael Collins was in the same block as Dad in prison'.

8 September 2003

I was born in Ballawinna, my parents were Sarah Monahan and Timothy Manning.

PAULINE: *– and Sarah Monahan was –*

A sister of Mrs Persse –

PAULINE: *That was Mary Monahan.*

Then there was Bridget, Mrs Keane, and there was Nora, Mrs Dooley in Kilchreest, and (*pause*) yes, that's it.

PAULINE: *So you were related to Frank Persse – Mary Monahan was your aunt.*

Mary Monahan was my aunt and she was married to Frank Persse.

PAULINE: *And you never met Mary – was she dead before you were born?*

Oh she was. But I remember her daughter, Alice, that who was married to the doctor in Limerick. I remember I was going to the National school. Her funeral came out to the station in Craughwell, the coffin came out there. And beautiful flowers, I remember that.

PAULINE: *And was there trouble the time they got married, do you think?*

Well there was, well there wasn't trouble like, but of course Mrs Persse didn't like it. Lady Gregory didn't mind I think, because she was very nice to Mary.

PAULINE: *You can name three of the children can you?*

I can name Alice, Millie and Sissy, and a boy Dudley was his name, and he was in the army, and he was killed very young.

PAULINE: *So when you were growing up did you speak much about Lady Gregory or –*

Well no, not that much. It does seem that there's a lovely statue of her in Craughwell, 'tis very nice, and hasn't she a beautiful place now, I was in the hotel called after her name, a few times.

PAULINE: *Have you been to Coole Park?*

No. And then, after they getting married, they lived in separate lodgings, as I told you, Frank hadn't his schooling finished, and after they getting married he had to go back to school again. And my mam used to tell me how she'd be sitting there, and she had all the neighbours doing the work. She'd be sowing corn and that, and she'd be sitting there like a lady on a Saturday night and she paying them all. So you see my mother must be fairly young when she was going to visit to her. If I could know where Mary came in in the family, I know that Mrs Keane was the oldest, and I think Mrs Dooley was next, but Mary must be next to Sarah, then my mother.

PAULINE: *You don't know when she died, no?*

I don't know the year, but I know she was only 42.

PAULINE: *And where did Frank Persse meet Mary?*

When she went to Roxborough, to the – sure he must be the man in Roxborough that I'm talking about, he must be William Monahan's brother, Martin, wouldn't he? I always heard him called the miller. Did he do milling?

PAULINE: *There was a mill there.*

Well she was sent there to write and read for him, when he was alone, and he had a housekeeper. But before that you see Frank Persse was engineering the pump in Ballywinna, he used to go to Templemartin, so I think that's where they sort of met first. But whenever after that then, they sent her to Roxborough and that's where they met finally then. And then he had a brother, what was the brother's name? I should know that. Persse – but anyway Frank used to go to the orchard of an evening and he used to bring cherries, and he used to go meeting Mary you see. So anyway the brother, I think 'twas Gerald, Gerald Persse, yeah, took off this evening after him, and he seen the two meeting. And he told the miller, I'll call him now, and immediately word was sent down to Temple-Martin, 'bring up her father and mother here', that she has to leave and go home. So finally they did, and the father and mother came to the mill, and Mary defied them that she would not go home, so Frank Persse was sent for. So Frank came, and they had a bit of an argument I think and he told them, 'Stay here till I come back'. And off he goes down to Kilchreest and got baptised. He was a Protestant you see. So now Mary was better to that – what else did he get done as well as getting baptised.

PAULINE: *So he converted to a Catholic so he could marry Mary?*

Yes. And then there was another story that my mother used to tell me. In Frank's – Frank's mother was so let down when he married a country girl that she lodged all his money or whatever money he was to get, in Australia. The two got married and they went to Australia on their honeymoon, and then they came back to Sycamore Lodge. And they lived in Sycamore Lodge until the family grew up, and then 'twas a bit small and they went to Lough Cutra. And I don't know much more. She died at 42. Sure I don't remember her at all.

MOLLY MURPHY *née* COEN

The editor's former National school teacher.
Martin Coen's sister.

I was born in Ballymaquive, in September 22, 1928. The youngest of a family of 8. And when I was four months old, as Martin told you, my sister contracted diphtheria and died, and my father got diphtheria. We were told that had he stayed at home he would have got over it, a big strong man, but they sent him to hospital and he got a chill on the way in so he developed pneumonia, so the two things together!

But my mother was left with seven then, and in those days farms didn't pay very well, and then she had no man to work the land. The eldest was my sister Dellie she was 12, all steps down along then to 4 months. But she was a marvellous woman, she never complained, she managed to work indoors and outdoors, sent us to school and helped us through lessons, it's amazing what she able to do. She was wonderful at housekeeping, she used to card wool – sheep's wool and knit jumpers, she was great at crochet and she made lots of dresses for us, we were never short of anything. And she was a great woman for gardening so we had loads of vegetables. We had a nice, happy life – she was a fantastic person. Then when each of us had our children she was by our side, helped us look after our children, Mat, his twelve, she was there to mind the children when Bridie was in hospital. She reared my three, when mine were born, when they first started school. She died in 1977 aged 84, she was Nora Glynn from Cahermore. Most of her brothers and sisters emigrated to America, so we have a lot of relations out there, and we still keep in touch with them all. I went out there a number of times and I met them, there was one particular occasion, all 30 of them came from all over the place just to meet their Irish cousin. I have a sister in Canada, Peggy, and she is in Toronto, so we are in contact with them all.

I won a County Council scholarship and I got 5 years free in the Convent of Mercy Secondary School. I was very interested in teaching all my life, ever since I was a child, secondary school of course, for university you could do Latin, French and that kind of thing, the preparatory schools then, they were more geared for the training college. But anyway when I came out after my Leaving Cert. it was just 1947, just after the war, and the first number were called to training in the county and then there were 18 or 20 appointed junior assistant mistresses and I was one of those. So at that time there seemed to be a great scarcity of teachers, because I can remember being offered 7 different schools at the time. I think the parish priests got a list of those who were on the list of J.A.Ms as they called them and they wrote to me, I didn't write to them. I decided on Donegal and I went there in 1947 and I stayed there until 1954. I loved it, I absolutely loved it, I was in the Gaeltacht, the Irish-speaking area, Glennfinn which 8 miles from Ballybofey, the only drawback was it took me 2 days to go there and 2 days to get back, believe it or not! A train from Ardrahan to Sligo on the first day, stayed there overnight and went by bus to Ballybofey the next day, then took the little narrow gauge train from Stranorlar to Glennfinn and cycled 3 miles after that. It was a beautiful place and all the children, they were all native Irish speakers and I had a wonderful Principal. He was an elderly man at the time and he had been born and reared there, and he had wonderful Irish, you would listen to him forever, he was educated in Derry, even though he belonged to Glenfinn, there was no training college in the area at the time, and his father had taught there before him. It was a one-roomed school for two teachers, it was very very big, big long seats, you know, whenever the seniors had any little noise that happened down the far end of the room, all my little ones would turn around and gaze at what was happening down below. I suppose they had a certain amount of difficulty understanding me because I had come from the west and they weren't accustomed to people from the west. I remember it was very funny one morning this little chap came into me, and he wasn't listening to what I was saying at all, and I said, 'You'll have to pay attention to me', he was looking back at the big brothers down the other end of the room. And he went home to his granny that evening and she said, 'What did the new teacher say to you'. 'Oh granny' he said, 'he said you'll have to pay her a pension!' I said attention. Another day it was rather funny, I was trying to explain to the children, living in Donegal, what were the other counties surrounding, and I said one day, I was trying to explain that they could go into Tyrone, or Sligo, or whatever or Derry, and they weren't getting the message anyway, and I said, 'well, if I were to leave Donegal now, where would I have to go? What's the next county I'd go to', and one little lad shot up his hand and said, 'Please miss, if you leave Donegal you'll have to go to the County Home'. I thought I was a bit too young for that, I was only about 23 or 4! But they were lovely children, and I was very, very happy there. I lived with a man and wife who had just got married, and I used to cycle across the bridge to the school. About a year and a half after I went there they opened a new school, a lovely two-teacher school, heaven on earth by comparison with the old. Then my mother went to New York and Canada in 1953 and she stayed a year there, she went out to my sister who was married there, and she had cousins down in New York, so I felt, well, I'll be back at school, and I won't see her for another year. So I applied for a school in Connemara, and I got it. Out in Recess, it was a two-teacher school in the fíor-Ghaeltacht, and I was delighted. It was a lovely school and I worked with a principal, he came from Clare. And we were very happy there too, because you didn't have to teach Irish there, or in Donegal. They came in, full of Irish, you know. They were as fluent in Irish as our children around here are in English. Then in 1959 I decided I'd come back home, if I were lucky enough to get a job. So I applied, and Mrs Burke was retiring in Kiltiernan, I applied for it, and got it. I spent 26 and a half very happy years there, lovely parents, lovely children, beautiful. And I was only four and a half miles from home so I took my children to school in the morning.

PAULINE: *And where did you meet the husband, then?*

I met him here at home – but I was about to tell you, I did the training course then in Mary Immaculate Training College, and I got my diploma then, it's a degree course now, and I was teaching then until 1984 when I had a car accident. And I went back a few times, but I wasn't able to raise my arms to the blackboard and I felt it wasn't fair for me to keep that, so I retired in 1985. I met my husband after I came home to teach, and I never – even though he came from the other end of the parish, I had never known him. And we went out together for about 8 months. Where'd I meet him first? I met him at the dancehall in Labane, and we seemed to just gravitate towards each other. So we have three children. Patrick, Martin and Nora, and we have them all around.

I loved the small children, I would never have liked to teach the senior classes, I was so used to infants first, that that is what I wanted, and I remember when I retired, before Martin's baby was born, I was lost, I was totally lost, and I used to go around the house, we'd just moved into this house here, and I'd spend my time thinking about what the infants were doing now – it's funny how you miss them. Now my own grandchildren come up to me every week and I love them coming in, and they're full of talk and full of chat and they talk to me about everything.

JOHN MOYLAN

my national school master
Kiltiernan National School
4 November 2003

*John was born in Rathcosgrove; his parents were John
Moylan, and Kathleen Linnane from Ballindereen. There
were seven children, five boys and two girls: he was 'more*

or less in the middle'. *He went to Ballyglass National School – teachers John Doyle and Mary Doyle. He finished at 13 and a half years, and went to St Mary's College in Galway. He won a scholarship to board there.*

There was supposed to be 6 scholarships in the county, most were given in Galway [*city*] as far as I know, I was the only one from the rest of the county who got a boarding scholarship. There weren't many boarders, maybe 60. In the '30s people were poor, they couldn't afford to pay boarding school fees, there were a few publicans' sons and shopkeepers' sons, a few teachers' sons, very few farmers' sons. We came home at Christmas and Easter.

He stayed 5 years in St Mary's. Then he went to Training College in St Patrick's, Drumcondra for two years. His first post was in Labane NS in 1940. Teaching was very hard work at that time, inspectors expected Irish spoken and written and taught and the grammar to do that was really hard work, also teaching English and catechism. He loved local history. John spent 2 years in Labane school the next place he went to was a school in Connemara, Leitir Mór, all Irish speaking.

Well, teaching there was hard too you didn't have to teach Irish but you had to try to teach English, and it wasn't easy, Connemara was very nice really except the school was overcrowded, sometimes two teachers in one room. Money was very scarce, this was during the war years and very little transport, hard even to get a bicycle tyre, travelling was localized. I stayed there for about two years then came back to Kiltiernan and stayed there until I retired.

PAULINE: *Why is Irish was so difficult to teach nowadays?*

The one good reason is the people are no longer interested in learning it, they think it is out of date and no use when they go out in the world, nobody will want to know about their Irish unfortunately. People like to know a certain amount particularly visitors from foreign countries want to know the meaning of place names. Ben Bulben why was it called this, they like to know the meanings for the mountains and lakes, the anglicized version of the Irish name, people like to know the history, why were they called. Why was Ardrahan called Ard Rath In, for example.

We all walked to school across the fields as did everybody, we walked to Mass you know, there were mass paths through the fields and a stile to get over the walls without knocking it, no one would prevent you from going in the path even though the land belonged to somebody. The Moylans went to Mass in Ballymana. Ardrahan was the parish church, Ballymana was part of the Craughwell parish but it was nearer than Labane, more convenient. People walked to Mass, young and old, the road would be black with people walking to Mass, some farmers had a sidecar and a horse. The first motorcar would have been in the '20s or '30s.

When we went to Mass we knew everybody in the chapel, we knew where they lived and where they came from, you would stand and talk outside the church, friendly. Nowadays people don't seem to know their neighbours and they certainly don't stand outside the church. They barely talk to one another.

Television changed people. A lot of people sit in and watch TV, don't go out and visit and tell old stories, they don't chat or laugh as much as they used to. Television is fine for news and sport.

People have lost the art of good storytelling. People used to make up good stories long ago, a good story teller came to visit, he would entertain everybody for an hour or so. There is not as much conversation in the house, children seem to be glued to the TV.

In most houses people knelt down and said the rosary every night, they don't do it now, I suppose it passed part of the night, an excuse to get everyone in, you knew where everyone was, it's gone in almost every house.

People worked very hard, but they didn't produce much with manual work, poor equipment, you would be a long time saving a few acres of hay, people cutting hay with a scythe, then they got the mowing machine, turn the hay with hay fork it would take a week to be ready to make it into little cocks, then brought into the haggard, make into a big sheep cock, so all that took a lot of time. The weather was never too suitable for harvesting, always a little too damp but people were happy doing it. They had most of their own food, people were fairly well fed, people walked a lot, they didn't have Wellingtons or rubber boots, people wore hobnailed boots. People didn't seem to go to the doctor only very occasionally. When I was young. I never went to the doctor, the doctor would come to the school annually.

People have developed an appetite for luxuries. When you are under those limestone crosses you will never count your gains or losses. It is not a bad policy to let the next generation do it for themselves. I think it helps in their development.

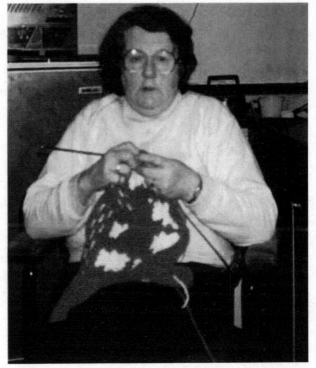

9 September 2003

PAULINE: *Kitty, where are you from originally?*

From Ballindereen. I was Kitty Moran. There was ten in
my family, four girls and six lads. There were five girls
but one of them died as a baby. I had a brother John
and he died at the age of 19, and he died of cancer of
the bone, he was next to me. Well, there was my brother
Pat, then there was a girl Katie she died, I had a sister
May, she was hit by a car, she lived six months, then

she died, then there was me, I was the fourth. There was Katie, May, me, Nellie, and Mary Ann. They're all dead now except Mary Ann. My father was a small farmer.

There was no work that time, no jobs, and I went to school, walked at that time, we wore no shoes in the summertime, that time, sore toes to the hard ground, we had a farm at home, and another small farm at Ard, we used have to go down there to milk the cows, and to take up the milk before we went to school, so I had to do that. We had no radios, we had no television. At night time, we used visit the neighbours, we used go to O'Connors, telling stories, and we enjoyed it often. So that's how we grew up. We started going to dances, there was snow, dancing in Johnston's Hall in Kinvara, 'twas for fourpence, fourpence to go in, if our parents had money to give us. There was no money in the country that time. There were no jobs. I learned a lot from my father. I worked out in the fields, I sprayed potatoes, I thinned beet, I pulled turnips, pulled mangolds, it was farming all the time. And then there were neighbours, Sweeneys we worked with them. They had a farm one side of us, I used to help them

PAULINE: *They'd give you some money would they?*

My mother, she needed it –

PAULINE: *And she'd give you money for the dance then would she?*

[*Laughs*] 'Twas fourpence at that time, the dance. But my father was, it wasn't that he was strict, but when he went in to do a job he'd do it, beet and swedes, that was lovely, we'd sit down on the headland and have a cigarette after every drill. We'd have the neighbours, great fun at night, but my father was sensible, you know, so, that was my youth, until, Labane Hall opened then, and I came a few times to Labane, we did often walk to Labane, we had no bicycle and it was during the war, trying to get petrol, it was a terrible time, trying to get the lads to fix the puncture, with the heat driving the patch they put on it would rise up again, and believe it or not, we had great fun. We enjoyed every minute of it you know. I think that television and all that has ruined the youth. We had no money but we had our own fun and we made it. And, we'd go to the dances and we'd have great fun. We'd walk the five miles to Ballindeeren four miles I suppose, a crowd of us together, the O'Connors and the Flannerys of the village, and we'd go there, and we'd dance every dance and we'd leave the dance and we'd walk home again. And we'd have a great night, I saw my daughters they'd have a seat to the dance and a seat back they'd come home, they were browned off when they got home. We had fun!

PAULINE: *And where would you get clothes that time?*

Oh we'd get clothes, we had to go to Galway to get the clothes. Or Kinvara. We had – we used make, my mother used make, she had a sewing machine that's how I learned to sew. That was years growing up, my brother died – I was married when he died, I married at about 19 I suppose.

PAULINE: *And where did you meet your husband?*

I met him in Ballindereen, he was threshing for John O'Mahony, Mike Mannion who was the postman here told me that he was the first man who ever drove a tractor in the parish of Ardrahan. So, John O'Mahony had a threshing machine, and Paddy went all over the place, in great demand threshing.That was the first place I met him. There was this guy – well I was young then, I was only fourteen and a half, didn't have much interest in boys at the time, this lad anyway he kept annoying me and he was on to me every chance he got, so Paddy was threshing and he was staying with this guy and this guy told him that he liked me, probably at my aunt's, because I used to visit my aunt, and he said, 'we'll go down' so the same day I worked a very hard day, I wasn't even dressed and I was sitting down there opposite the house, they had hobs on the house, sitting on the hob, my aunt Winnie was churning, making butter, and she went out, and she said, 'Kitty wake up' she said, 'I saw two cigarettes coming down the boreen' she said, 'one of them is a small one' she said, 'and the other is a big one' she said. So they came in anyway, that was the first time I saw him, he was a very quiet man, he was a gentleman from the first day I ever knew him until the day he died. So we were talking, well I wasn't talking to him anyway, the other guy was talking, but he was talking to my grandmother. God rest them all, they're all gone. So I was very tired and I had a message to pick up from my aunt that was why I was there at the time, so she gave me the message, and my brother John, who was with me that night, so I said, 'I'm going home'. So I stood up to go, they stood up too, it was ten o'clock, I said, 'Good night' and we had a good go from here to Lowry's, out the boreen to the main road, and John said to me, 'They're coming'. I knew well who was coming. So, we got out to the main road anyway, and I said, 'Goodnight' and I turned towards Ballindereen and they could have gone the other way, going two different ways, next thing was, they came after me again, so it wasn't the tall fella it was the small fella, so he made a grab for me to go talking to me and I wasn't interested in talking,so then he walked off with my brother John and he left the tall fella to chat me for him. So he tried all right, and he asked me about the other fella would I make it up with him, I said, there's nothing to make up anyway, that it was all in his own head –

PAULINE: *What age were you this time now?*

I was only about fourteen and a half. Oh I was very tall for my age, nobody would have believed it. So we got near the village anyway then he said, 'Would you come out to meet me if I asked?' I said ok. So we made a date for Sunday night, but Sunday night I remember it well, he was at a card game on the Friday night and he met a friend of mine, she said that he was lovely, lovely-mannered fellow, and she said, 'He has a date with you Sunday night', so I said, 'it's very doubtful if I'll be there'. 'Oh God', said she, 'you won't do that'. 'If you're so interested, go there you', I said. 'I couldn't do that', she said. I was to meet him in Clogh, my father sent me to Ard on a message, I went to Ard for the message, and I had to come from Ard, and I didn't get to Clogh at the time, so that night there was a card game at Trotters – Bogtrotters we used to call it – 'twas Joe Connors that started that, so the priest had a sermon that morning, what do you call, children – thought that they were crippled, polio, 'twas raging that time, three children of the parish got it, the priest said to keep away from crowded places, so I was advised not to go to Connors that night, of course my mother was a very strict-to-obey lady, 'Are you going there?' so John and I linked arms and went dancing in at Connors, and sure, we went in, and as soon as I arrived there I was asked to dance, so I was dancing, and there were strangers there. They had a cardgame, and dancing in the kitchen, so this girl came up to me and she said, 'Do you see who's inside the door', I'm not so sure because I was half-asleep and I said, 'yes I do', and she said, 'you should talk to him'. I said, 'probably', so when he came back anyway, I went up to talk to Paddy beside the door and my brother John came back so I said to Paddy I have to go, so he said, 'I'll walk you over the road', and they were, 'Paddy, where is the child'.

PAULINE: *What age was Paddy this time?*

He was ten years and six months older than me. He was twenty-four/twenty-five. He asked me what age I was and I said, 'what difference does it make', so I didn't tell him. He really thought I was … so then I was only 19 when we got married.

14 February 2004

PAULINE: *Your right name is John? And where did you get the name Lowry?*

From hurling.

PAULINE: *And who gave it to you?*

Pateen Shaughnessy.

PAULINE: *And why did you get that name? Were you a good hurler?*

Oh I suppose I was middling, middling. Fair. I was named for Lowry Maher, Kilkenny, I suppose. And it stuck to me then. I was never called John, only Lowry. There was a lot of nicknames that time. Carthy Coen Dinny Murray the Lord have mercy on him, his name was Peadar, Paraic Diviney, Clasby they used to call him – I don't know [*laughs*]. That was our hurling team like, our '49 team.

PAULINE: *And did you win that year?*

We did, we won the cup. Only one year we won it. One or two more years we joined with Gort and they were no good to us.

PAULINE: *And where were you born Lowry?*

I was born in Turceen in Connemara, outside Roundstone. I came to Tulira when I was only one year old, father, mother and seven children. He was a ganger. They had a pub in Roundstone, Ballinafad, Nee's pub. So I was only a year old when I came to Kiltartan – as you go up to Gort. We were there for about two years, and we came to Tulira. The gate lodge. My father worked in Tulira first, for Edward Martyn. Anyone that worked in it, they got to buy the land, thirty-five acres. We all got a bit.My father and Junior Mahony worked together, ganging. For the Land Commission. I went to school to Mrs Fahy and Tommy O'Meara.

PAULINE: *Did you like school?*

I did, I liked Mrs Fahy and I spent about a month with Old Flanagan. Mrs Fahy was a long time teaching. Oh I had a lot of teachers. I had Fenton. He was a Kerryman. So I was in this school here, around Kelly's saddle shop in Ardrahan, for two and a half year. I'd be around 15. Oh I spent two and a half year or more with him, Lord have mercy on them all. Then we went on to the beet – your daddy was forking beet with me in Ardrahan – and then went into Tulira in 1949. And I was there till '86. I was active in Tulira, between Oranmore, her own place in Ballinrobe, that is Mrs Hemphill Mount Armstrong, Kildare – they were all their farms – so I was there with Mrs Braden the Lord have mercy on her in Tulira, I was there with Henry the Yank Brown, he died of cancer, and I finished with Mrs Braden, went into Galway after. When she came to Tulira first I was with her for eight or nine months in the castle and Mayo. So she went to Dublin, hospital in January, she died in March. She was lovely, lovely, done up to the nines as far as the last. So Brown came then, he was American, he was married to a girl from Headford, Carey girl. He died of cancer.

PAULINE: *What famous people did you see coming to Tulira?*

Oh sure our late Taoiseach's [*daughter*], Eimear Haughey, Charlie's daughter, was reared in Tulira. Sure she was hunting with them the whole time. And Charlie was there in summertime. John Huston, sure they were there. I wouldn't know, I was gone the whole time.

But I suppose in the early days we were wild. We were called the Moscows. There was a good eight. There was Sean Niland, the Quinns, there was three of us in it, Paddy, Dinny and me, Jack Quinn the Lord hav mercy on him, Ned Quinn, Paraic Diviney Johnny Diviney, and we had Dick Ryan he was working in Gilligans. But games of cards we used to go, and cross-country, knocking walls that weren't too high! [*laughs*]. Oh sure your father was in it too. Why wouldn't he. They were coming from far and near. Pitch and toss we had then we had – we made a penny with two heads, – that was going on every Sunday, because we couldn't lose, we had a penny with two heads. Made it on the railway, under the railway track.

I will tell you when John Moylan came to Labane first teaching, myself and Bill Joe the Lord have Mercy on him, we had a game of Pontoon, we had the cards docked, we took £21 one Sunday after second mass anyhow there was a Marquee in Oranmore that night we were ready to go, 3 of us, sure went to Taylors first before we went down on bikes, we weren't so very long there when Bill Joe was going to be put out of the Marquee, it was about 2 o'clock in the morning I helped him anyway and got a hammer too and fled the 2 of us, we cycled away the 2 of us coming up around 4 o'clock in the morning.

I never got married; I went through too many of them, too many I seen in me time. In Kildare they were like flies coming out from Dublin on a Friday night. I had another lad with me, a Galway man, he got married to a Wicklow girl.

I was born 4th February 1921.

12 January 2004

I was born the 13th of February 1916, registered in
Loughrea as the 27th. They'd be fined a pound or
something if you left the child go over three months, do
you see. The nurse didn't do it, the nurses do that now,
but they didn't do in my time like, and one of the
parents would have to go to Loughrea to register the
birth, and when a baby was born, if the weather would
be bad, neither my father nor my mother travelled by
bicycle, they had to go by horse and cart, they had no

other means of going, and the weather was bad and they didn't go in time, they left me a bit older than I was. I was born at home; there was no such thing as the women going to hospital that time, we were all born at home seven of us, with Nurse McCarthy, you would have heard of her, and Dr. Tim I think for Tommy, he was the oldest and the nurse after that then. There was no hospital at all. The women stayed in bed for a week. at least. And there was no such thing as a bath. I was born in a thatched house, houses were small, there'd be three children sleeping in the one bed. There could be three generations in one house; my grandmother was there, my father's mother was there when I was there first, but I was nearly two months old, I heard them saying, when she died. I was born in February, and she died the following April, and I know they said that she asked for me to be left up to the bed to her, before she died, and shortly afterwards she died, so then my father was a good bit older than my mother too, it seems you see they didn't build a house like they do now, the young people moved in with the old people, I suppose the old woman didn't want to give up her – authority [*laughs*], she got very old so, that was the way things happened then, my father was 50 I think, my mother was a good bit younger, I don't know how many years younger –

I was the second. Tommy was the oldest, 89 now this month if he lived, he died last May. At 88. And Simon was next, my father got pneumonia then. Paddy was the youngest he was eight years younger than me, and hardly had he been born when my father got pneumonia, and he was in bed, oh I suppose, six weeks anyway, but he wasn't able to do much that year, so mother had to – I know I was minding Bertie and Paddy, the youngest, during the summer and the eldest would be out working, helped out by the neighbours and that. The neighbours were great. Then my father got out of that pneumonia then and he got cancer, God help us, eight years after that. He died in 1933 anyway. I was 17, Paddy was 8 years, and Tommy and Simon then, the two eldest boys, they had to work very hard, that was a bit of a struggle, to rear us I suppose. Small farm and bad prices for stock at the time, there wasn't so much stock at the time, though the farm was small, they didn't have a lot of stock.

My mother was from Ballindereen, she was Heneghan. Her brother got a place, 'twas divided and he had I suppose nine or ten children and they're all dead now, except for two girls, the eldest and the youngest. And the second boy he had got the farm and he never got married, he left it to a nephew in Australia, he'd be Heneghan I suppose he wanted to keep up the family name, sure Heneghan didn't stay in it, he sold it, and there's no-one in it. The eldest girl is married to a man from Co. Tyrone, she had three children, two boys and a girl. And the youngest girl then, she was married and living in Co Monaghan, and she had a big family.

I went to school in Ballyglass, to Mr Doyle, he was a very good teacher too. But I had bad luck. Mr Doyle was to put me on for, the County Council scholarship, he said that I was one of the best he taught in a good year, I had the most – oh I could pick up things fast. He put me in for the scholarship. I was a few months too old, he should have put me in the year before that … but he used to say that I was a very brainy girl, very intelligent. Then you see, I was born of poor parents, they weren't able to pay for me to put me through school, and I had to take tough work. My mother didn't want me to England, and I always wanted to be a nurse, so I couldn't get a job locally. I answered an ad in the paper one time and I was called to Dublin. 'Twas a country shop outside Dublin, 'twas a place called the Naul, and she was a tough sort of a woman, she had a grocery shop and she had a – pub, but I never was asked to work in the pub, but I was in the grocery, it wasn't a very busy shop. It was north county Dublin, not so far from Balbriggan and I spent a year there, and she had a sister married across the road, she had a post office and shop, she had a girl working for her and she was leaving, and she asked me, had I a sister, I said I had but, I'd go myself actually! [*laughs*]. So I started doing post office work! So I went in to her and she was a very nice woman altogether, and I was only about a year there and I saw an ad in the Catholic paper I used to get from England, *The Universe*, and I saw this ad where they were looking for nurses in this fever hospital, and I'd get £40 a year, and if I went for general I'd only get £30, so I said that I'd try for fever nurse first so I tried, and I was called to London and I done the fever – I went in 1937, I was just gone 21, but my mother didn't want me to go to London, at all, and I went in 1937, 'twas a two-year's course, and it was – about to sit my finals in October, and war broke out in September 1939 and the exam was delayed until the following February. I sat the following February and I got my exam, and doing general then I went to the North Middlesex, 'twas the Middlesex County Council, and I could do my general in two years when I had the fever [*training*], so I had just my year done when they told me I could go home on holidays. I put in the Blitz, the war, the planes going over every night, you could see nothing, we were moved out the country a bit then, you see, to other hospitals, one was a mental hospital but they made part of it for general, they wanted to bring the nurses and the patients out of London because the jerries as they used to call them they were watching the hospitals if they could they'd bomb some of them. I went out anyway to Essex first, and I spent a while there, back again and I went to the Middlesex and served my time there and in 1941 they told me it was holidays, because I got no holidays from 1938, this was 1941. I went home on holidays in 1941 and – met with Michael Niland. And never went back [*laughs*].

PAULINE: *Did you ever regret not going back?*

Well I did, I always wanted to be a nurse, you see, I said, 'will I go and be killed, for England' but ...

PAULINE: *Love won out. And where did you meet himself?*

Oh in Labane, in a hall? Well I did meet him before I was home another time, last time I was home and he was, by the way, making out to me that I was going out with somebody else at the time, and we fell out, before any – this is the way it went, and I'm – 62 years married now, married in 1941, I'm 62 years married since last April, next April I'll be 63 years married. We got married in Labane, went away for honeymoon, and I was working from then on and I didn't get any rest, worked hard, feeding gangs for him when he was cutting timber and started the garage. We always lived here; his mother and father were here, the two of them, when I came but I was only one month here when his mother got a stroke and she died, well I – I was a month here when she got the stroke, she lived a bit – the father lived on then, he lived a long time here, he was thirty years with me, he died in the 1970s, she died in the 1940s, so wasn't it a bit of a distance between the two of them. So Mike died in '97.

PAULINE: *You must have had a lot of characters around here with the garage though.*

Great old fun. Dr Joyce used to come in here, came in one day with the lawnmower, he said, 'you'd think 'twas flying the Atlantic you'd be with it'. But before that Dr – who was the man before him, he was an awful nice man altogether, from Loughrea I think, O'Beirne yes, he was lovely, we used to have great fun with him here, he had an old sports car here one time, he had it left out there in front of a wall or something and some cow eat a bit of – not plastic, it wasn't plastic, the soft top of it, Michael Sheehan worked here, he was great gas altogether, we used to have great fun. With Michael. And Leo Guilfoyle of course, great fun, the two of them would come there in the morning, on the motorbike, Leo had a motorbike.

PAULINE: *What's the biggest change, now, you can see around, with people?*

Well, that time people they went to visit oftener to each other, I don't know but they talked more to one another, they haven't time to talk to you now, busy with the television and all this crack, the people were a lot friendlier, they used to gather – we used have a few local lads here playing cards, but you don't see that at all now, it used to pass the night, but you don't see neighbours going in and out now.

At Christmas, we didn't have as many toys as they have now, that's for certain. We were delighted with a few little things, very much delighted to go to visit to the neighbours the next house, there was three or four houses near us, we'd get a drop of wine or a drop of mineral or something and a bit of sweet cake, and sure we thought that was great.

There would be, a few neighbours working abroad in shops, coming home at night, not many had jobs really and truly there was a good deal of grownups and they had no jobs, they worked with their father, 20s and 30s was very bad times, you couldn't get a job anywhere, I was glad when I reached 16 or that, I could go to America, then you see, but 'twas bad that time, they wouldn't allow you go to America, because America was suffering from a bad time themselves, the banks closed down, a lot of people, they wouldn't allow you out. Then I had to wait. only that I got that little job in Dublin sure, it wasn't much to get, but 'twas a job and I was thinking it would maybe come to something better after a while, [*hard to make out*], then England, a lot of Irish girls went there.

PAULINE: *How many children did you have?*

Three boys; Kevin, Anthony and Vincent.

July 2003

TOM: I was born within a shout of the whole place, Augusta Persse was born 15th March 1852 in a country house called Roxborough, Co Galway. She was the youngest daughter of Dudley Persse, who at one time owned an estate nearly 4000 acres. So the people wanted the land divided and they didn't want her to be owning it. In the 1880s she married Sir William

Gregory whose house and property were Coole Park. We're only a few miles from it. Sir William had a varied and interesting career. As a young man he was a devotee of the turf, which is horse-racing, and he had to sell thousands of his Irish acres to pay his debts, he got broke. He became the notable and well-beloved governor of Ceylon. His autobiography originally printed only for his friends' eyes is one of the most honest I have read. He died in 1892. Augusta Persse was his second wife. He had no issue by his first wife. By his second he had one child, Robert, who became a distinguished painter, and met his end flying over Italy during the war of 1914–18.

Her husband was buried in Coole Park ... the Dooleys and the Hehirs, they carried his coffin across the fields, they came to the head of the road, and they carried the coffin. It was a lead-lined coffin and they carried it, there were about ten of them, down the fields, half a mile down from the main road, he was buried there. We heard when his son was killed in an air crash.

They built a school in Kiltartan, the government provided a grant, but the Gregorys paid the rest of the money. 1960 there was a new school built, but I went to the old school.

PAULINE: *And was Lady Gregory ever mentioned there?*

TOM: There was never much mention of her, like, but she was pretty good enough, in the parish, she used to send over apples to the school, and she was very good to Malachy Quinn during the time that the wife was murdered, shot, on her doorstep. She wrote letters to the British authorities looking for compensation for Malachy Quinn and I think he got £300, which was a lot of money in those days. She was good like that too. I never saw her, her funeral passed by the old school, we were all only 7 or 8 years at the time, we didn't take much notice of her.

From Gort we'd come down and we'd go in walking to Coole, at that time the house had not been lived in fir many years no doors or windows in it, there's a few old statues in it, we never bothered, or were interested in it. In those days people turned their back on that kind of stuff, 'twould be different if 'twas nowadays, people had no interest but in those days they couldn't be bothered. Coole House was a fine building, but there was no great quality stone in it, a lot of it when 'twas demolished, farmers took some of it for building walls, and any good stone was brought – at the time they were building the new church in Portumna, and there were some few lorryloads of stones taken for the building of the church there.

PADDY: There were orchards, we often went to great trouble climbing very high walls to get in for a feed of apples, but if Paddy Hehir caught you, he was working there, you could be in big trouble, but we were young and we were well able to run and get away from him.

The Loughnane brothers were threshing their mother's corn in Shanaglish, and Tans surrounded them, so they ran, I think one of them got away, he was crossing the graveyard, and didn't he trip and fall, and the bullet struck the headstone in front of him so he got away. The two brothers, they were dragged behind the lorries and they were brought and they were beaten to death below there, brought to Drumarsna Castle where there was a battalion of Black and Tans in it, and brutally murdered there, and the next thing was, they brought them and they dumped them into a pond of water there for a few days, and they were wandering around Gort looking for them, telling people that they escaped and enquiring of where they were, and they having them murdered, and it was some fellow who was watering cattle in an old pond that spotted them. They were brought back into Kinvara by IRA people, neighbours there, brought in the bodies and they were buried in the new cemetery in Shanaglish.

Patsy on left
7/11/2003

I went to school in Killeeneen for 2 years anyway and maybe more I went to school in Ballyglass then. I was born here where you are sitting. This house is shoving up nearly 100 years. My father is from Clare, Carron, you could say, and my mother came from Killeeneen.

PAULINE: *Where did they meet?*

I suppose they didn't meet – but someone met them! Someone down in Kileeneen a cousin of the O'Deas – made the match. Dan Furey was his name.

PAULINE: *How come they ended up living here?*

Well my father – the land was divided around here it was all one before that – a first cousin of my father,

Hynes, he wasn't very interested in it and sold it to my father then and he went off to England and made a lot of money in England or off to America made a lot of money over there.

PAULINE: *Your father died when you were very young?*

I was four years in March and he died in April, Pneumonia that time and there was no right cure for it. I went to school maybe between 4–5 years, there was school in the village of Killeeneen that time and that's where I started off anyway, and 1914 they had a new school.

PAULINE: *What year were you born?*

March 2nd 1909. I was seven years when I came up anyway, the book that came from Ballyglass, I was 7 years I don't know rightly it might be 7 and a half it might be after the holidays I started. Mrs Doyle was the teacher and she died fairly young, she used to teach me after I went to Ballyglass and then Mr Doyle teaching me for the rest of the time I spent in school I left it at 14, I worked at home, there was nothing else to be got much at that time. Well I worked down in Castletaylor then for a time. I worked in it a couple of different times and I worked along that road now from along over as far as McTigues there. In Castletaylor I was working in the garden, there was a big garden there, it was gone wild, digging it up I didn't mind. 24 shillings it wouldn't be much good now – 4 shillings a day. Shaw Taylor he sold the place and went out to Africa.

PAULINE: *What year did you get married?*

1930 I think … I was 22. The month of April the 16th of April. I met her in her own home, well she was only about a mile down from Killeeneen, about a mile from Killeeneen to Lavally. I spent four years going up and down and it was a long journey but I had the bike so it wasn't too bad. Married in Clarinbridge.

PAULINE: *Where did you go for your honeymoon?*

Came home here and that was the honeymoon, saving spuds the following day!

O we went to Galway the day we got married. I suppose we were walking around. Willie Quinn in Labane that brought us to Galway, he went home and collected us again. Money was scarce – money wasn't plentiful that time. The rent we used to be paying that time was going over to England, De Valera got in and he started the Republic of Ireland, he stopped the rent and kept it here in Ireland. England got us back then, they used to be buying a lot of cattle here do you know, cattle got awful cheap because they wouldn't buy them then and there was a few years then like that fairly bad.

PAULINE: *How many children did you have?*

Seven children and one died. He was about 8 months when he died.

ANN O'NEILL

Born in Killeenavarra and went to school in Ballindereen; 6 girls and 1 boy. Her mother died aged 35. She finished school.

I didn't stay too late to tell you the truth. I stayed at home working on the farm. It was my job to look after the horses, harrowing. My brother was the baby when our mother died – John, died and buried long ago.

I was in England when I was 19 years of age, housekeeping, cooking, working in the kitchen. At conscripting age I went to the factory and I worked for one week on a filling machine – filling little detonators; there would be 15 in every tunnel and I worked behind a shield making powder – it was very explosive the highest you could get – you wouldn't be allowed to wear rings or slides in your hair, after a short time I was asked if I would like to go on maintenance, sure I jumped at it, sure Pauline; I didn't know I was on such a dangerous job. A week later I was sorry, so I went to my Blue Band [*superviser*] and said I wouldn't like to go because I wouldn't know any girls coming from all over England, but I had to go as I had signed up. In a couple of weeks we were all loaded up in a bus and went to a place called Wigan near Bolton, into a big orphanage, that is where we were staying, a row of beds, army beds and army blankets. Then we would go off to the place we were shedding, the maintenance filling machine, fill the powder with so much pressure on it it was our job to take off the press heads when they would fire and replace it again with a new press head. Then we would put on an internal cleaner that was for cleaning the detonators when we were finished with that we were put on an external cleaner, next put on a rotary machine, we weren't paid until we were trained. Next a varnishing machine detonators had to be varnished. – a detonator is a little brass affair with little caps on the top of it, you press down the cap for putting on the big bombs. Well I wasn't much good to tell you the truth. I was very great with this girl Eunice Marsh was her name and we became great friends she helped me a lot. We came back to Crow Lane, a long examination by Mr Radcliff, he had lost fingers I noticed and he put us through our paces what we learned while we were there.

We had a navy blue overall with a drop back, navy cap and my band with P.M.M 'Poor Maternity Mothers' they used to call us, but we were Process Machine Mechanics, so then I had a couple of years on

Group 1, getting too smart for our job so we were moved on to a bigger group.

I came home to Ireland very little during the war – we had to carry our gas masks and ear plugs, we didn't come that much as I had a bad experience when I was going over, the night before there was a ship coming into Larne I think was that was bombed with a big loss of lives, it must be 1940. When I was at home the people I was working for, the morning I was going out to England, rang Keanes saying, 'Stay at home until further notice' and when I went to Athenry there was another phone call for me telling me to stay at home, God I did, I was 6 months at home before I got the call to go back, I was working for the family then and they moved from London to Buckinghamshire when they got the house in Buckinghamshire they sent for me. The man in the house said he didn't have a right meal since I went back to Ireland.

When I came back to Ireland I went up to Keanes in Cahermooneen to visit, who the dickens did I meet but Sis Joyce and I said to her, 'By the way how is Eugene O'Neill', she said 'I must tell him you were asking', but he came down the following Sunday night to Killeenavara cross and I wasn't there; if I didn't marry I might never stand in Killeenavara again, my father and mother had such *meas* on Eugene. I used to meet him going around with the post, he asked me to marry him.

I heard the banshee since I came here the night Kathleen Keane died. I remember the flowers were beautiful out there in the front and it was nine o'clock in the evening and I heard great crying. Another night I was in Toureen I was reading cards, I blame that for it, we were reading fortunes, we went off on the bicycles, we came out on the Tarea road. The tailor

Connell, the tailor was an invalid, I went as far as her [*Kathleen's*] house, and I had a lovely coat, fur, and it started to make a shower big drops, and I came off the bicycle and went under a bush and I saw the woman with the long hair, sitting in front of me and when I came in home that night my aunt said, the Lord have mercy on her. Another night in the very self and same spot the chain of the bike came out and I couldn't put it in if I died, I was so excited.

I got married in 1943, September, I am 60 years here. Mrs Bermingham and Sis Joyce used to come here to visit me, Sis would be all the time smoking, I never smoked when I was in England. Sis would always say 'Anne come on and have one', then I started. I would have the fag in the mouth waiting for the kettle to boil. I was a long time looking out the window, it was a big change from England.

2 December 2003

From Ballinduff, Edward called Nedd Four boys and three girls in his family growing up; two are dead, one is in England, the rest are in the area. All went to school in Labane. Tommy O'Meara was the teacher, a Tipperary man, a great hurler in his day.

PAULINE: *Did he get you hurling?*

He did. He was a great man promoting hurling in the school, we were trying to be good, we were.

PAULINE: *Did you play for Galway?*

Yes I did, 1950–1954. We won the League and we won the Oireachteas a couple of times, that was all we won, we won no All-Ireland and we won no Railway Cup, they won the Railway Cup the year before I went to play.

When we were young lads we would spend the whole day hurling and then when we got bigger and grew up a bit, when we came to 16 and 17 and that we would play 'Pitch and Toss' down there at Murray's gate, Hemphill's gateway there. We would be pitching on the road that would be late, we would have enough of hurling.

Then there was a mob of us together and we would be going here there and everywhere. We would walk across the country too, up to Kennedys in Limepark, up along, up across all the way.

We won a gramophone, we were coming home anyway and said we would rest the gramophone, we left it up on the pier of a gate – put on a tune and came away home. We had great fun, that's all dead and gone. We had great fun up until our twenties, and sure we had no money and we were as happy as Larry. Every young lad today has a fist of money, if you hadn't money you don't get into drinking or rowdyism or anything and drink that causes the rowdyism, as far as I can see.

I remember as well as rain, could be going off to Gort to an old dance or marquee. I had the price of the marquee, I mightn't have a shilling or two shillings left, you had no more money than that.

I remember hurling with the county and only had a fiver going, a fiver. We weren't doing much drinking I don't know what kind of craze come into the youth that they took to drinking, it is a sadness, they think there is no enjoyment without drink. Young people nowadays have not the same fun.

I was born in Ballinasloe, then when my father got into bad health we came to Ardrahan, and I was reared with an aunt in Castletaylor.

I went to school in Kiltiernan, my teachers were John Moylan and Mrs Burke [*laughs*]. I didn't go too long now, to tell you the truth, but they were bad years sure.

PAULINE: *And how did you get involved in the drama?*

Ah I don't know how I got involved in it, I suppose my father and the masters both joined, Jack

[*Shaughnessy*], they'd have been up in Jack's house, that's where their play was rehearsed, Jack's house every night, every Saturday mighty then, Canon John [*Considine*] was alive that time, he gave us the hall for seven weeks I think, himself and Jack was in the throes all the time, they never got on but, the night of the play the hall was packed.

PAULINE: *Somebody told me there were a thousand people?*

There must be, so 'twas great, we went a few more places with it, Craughwell, oh we used have great fun, it was great. But he wrote another one before that, I think Mary Bradley was in it, they're nearly all dead now, Mike Quinn was in it, Tom Leech was in it. I don't know did they do that in many places. We did another one again. I think that was 'Trouble in Castlebell'. So great old time.

PAULINE: *Would you rehearse them often then?*

Every night we'd meet in Jack's. Oh jeez it used to be terrible. Ten or twelve in the kitchen and – he was great in a way like. He used to write the plays. Then the play would be on for the one night, and they'd come from all over. This must be 1952 or 3, I suppose, around that time. An English man, he used to work on the council that time. 'Road worker turns to playwright' was the headline. He [*Jack Shaughnessy*] got a great write-up on it. He was a great old character. Ah we enjoyed it. It was great. The rehearsing of it like – when the play is over the crack is gone. There was no other place to go.

2 September 2003

Angela was born in Ballylinn, Craughwell, in 1913.

PAULINE: *What was your maiden name?*

O'Shaughnessy, there were five boys and five girls in the family. I went to Ballymana National School until I was fourteen and then went to Loughrea secondary school where I was a boarder for 4 years.

PAULINE: *That was unusual that time.*

It was unusual there were only 3 doing the Leaving Cert. It was kind of the beginning of education. I was the only one to go boarding, three of my sisters entered the convent, two of them died young,one died at 6 years of meningitis and another at 18 from meningitis, and 3 of the girls entered the convent, another sister got married and I married.

PAULINE: *Did they stay in the convent?*

Yes they did, the last one alive is 91, she had her hip done 4 years ago. She didn't want to get it done, she got a stroke immediately afterwards which left her paralysed. She lives in Newry in Glenvale convent. I go to see her now and then, but it is very far away.

PAULINE: *Did you ever think of entering the convent?*

No, never.

PAULINE: *What did the lads do?*

One of them went for the priests, the other fellows stayed at home. The priest was twenty-five years in Africa and twenty years in America, he died in January or February, in the North. When I left school I looked for a job, that was in the 30s, economic depression, I could not get a job so I stayed at home, I tried everything, no such thing as a job that time. I didn't want to go away as my mother was there, so that was it I never got an advantage for my education. I worked around the house cooking and cleaning and I was happy. We had great times dancing; dancing all the time, dancing and playing in every house, we could have a dance every night. In every house someone was able to play and dance; we had dances sometimes every night of the week.

PAULINE: *What kind of music?*

Accordion and violin, céilí music of course sets, eight-hand reels, the Stack of Barley, barn dances, they don't know how to dance nowadays. I was in Craughwell dance hall the night it opened, we opened it we had drama a dramatic society in Craughwell, Fr O'Donoghue started it and we opened the hall with it. All I remember it was St Patrick's night it must be sixty years ago, we used to have plays and concerts we used to have great fun. We put plays on all over the county, we did comedy and all sorts.

I met my husband at a dance in Craughwell he was from Ardrahan six or seven miles away. Well I thought he was lovely them, but I didn't want to get married. I was happy as I was. I put it off, my brother he was home from Africa, he was been sent to America, he insisted I get married before he left, otherwise I would be hanging on another while. After a while we moved to Ardrahan, we had three girls. Cora the eldest was born Christmas night, we had two more daughters. We had 80 acres, I never worked on it, I didn't think it was a woman's job, I never had to anyway. Mick was a good worker, every evening he came in, washed, shaved and dressed up, and went visiting or went to a meeting; he was a perfectionist in everything he did. The farm was perfect gates and walls; he was a great worker but did not kill himself. He quit in the evening at six or six-thirty and cleaned up. He was always involved in GAA he never missed an All-Ireland in 80 yrs or 70 something. Anyway, he died when he was 92 and was at the All-Ireland that year, he went on the train, he had to go to the matches, I didn't mind, I didn't go, I had my friends here, we had parties. I didn't want to go to matches I went once to Croke Park. We used to go to GAA dances in the Warwick hotel [*in Salthill*], he didn't dance but I did. I would sing Danny Boy. I lost my voice when I got married, I had nothing to sing about after that. If you don't practice you lose your voice.

We were very happy married, I never had to worry. You didn't need much that time. No such thing as a mortgage and I made all the children's clothes, I had a poultry farm I used to supply eggs. I had about 200 hens, self-sufficient. People don't do anything now. I had incubators, used sell eggs all over the county. It's sad my granddaughter never saw a day- old chick. They don't want small supply farms anymore, they got so big, supply all. Supply farms they used to call us, and they died out. The poultry instructress would call out testing see everything was fine, we always had fresh eggs, and good eggs. We managed; I never seemed to be in debt, we always had enough.

My mother died in 1957, my father died in 1948, he was 80, she was 78, my brother never married, sold the farm, eventually died. They are all gone, where do the years go? I don't know what I am waiting for, why will He not take me. I don't know would you call it happy? It is ok when you can manage on your own but after that I don't want to be dependent on anyone.

One daughter lives in Mayo, one in London, and one in Cork, so they can't come that often, but that is fine. I'd be gone long ago if I had a son, he would be married and the wife would want to get rid of me. Cora my eldest went to Taylor's Hill boarding, the other two went to Gort, but they are all ok, married and useful.

When I was in boarding school I came home at Christmas and Easter, my family could visit me once a month. If you were out for a walk and you met someone on the street you could not talk to them, you could not talk to anyone out town. I enjoyed school but I was glad to be out of it in the finish. We had a mistress of rules we were frightened to death of her, she never smiled, she opened our letters going out and coming in. I remember my brother writing to me one time, I still have it. He wrote it so tiny that they could not read it, he did this in order to handicap them so they could not read it. They were very strict, it was alright in spots. I was glad when we finished. We had to work hard of course.

PAULINE: *What subjects did you do?*

Irish, English, History, Geography, Science and drawing, I was better off with an education, it was ok, but it was so strict it was outrageous. I got seven honours in the Leaving but I could not go to university. I stayed at home and worked and waited for a husband I suppose, I wasn't very keen on that either. I kept putting it off as long as I could. I loved dancing and going to parties, no such thing as what goes on nowadays.

29 March 2004

Journeymen were like 'kings of the road'.

PAULINE: *Were they travellers?*

No they were a better class, they were very good, good farriers they also did other work at particular times of the year there would be ploughs and harrows.

PAULINE: *Would they move around from place to place?*

Yes they would, there was one man that used to come here in my father's time. He would walk in out of the road looking for work. No problem, there was plenty of work, he might stay 2 or 3 months – we'd look after him and feed him. He was a great farrier – a wonderful farrier, he had a kind of photographic memory, he could make a set of shoes for a horse, leave them up there and a name on them. I heard my father saying one time he left – he would walk – he would come along on a fine day and say I am off, and there could be ten horses outside the door to be shod, it made no difference, he was going and that was it, maybe off to Kerry or somewhere else and went to another man and work there for another couple of months and he might leave and go somewhere else. Kind of nomads in their own way, no fixed abode if you like, and very good at their job. That man was very good – he was Sheedy – on foot and a little bag of tools, he would have a hammer and a couple of tongs under his arm, tools of the trade, he left one and he had 20 or 30 sets of shoes left up on the wall ready to go on and you would have very little to do with them. There were a number of them on the road and he was one of them. I often heard my father talking about him and I think there were men before that. They were the same in my grandfather's time.

My grandfather, as I told you before, did work for all the landlords around and all the gentry around. The Persses of Roxborough, Lady Gregory's ancestors. There were 2 Persses, Burton, I forget the other fellow, one was called Major Persse. In Roxborough they had 3 teams of horses. Six horses they had to be shod, he had to do one day a week there himself, he had men working for him as well. We cycled or went in a pony and cart. The coal would be in the yard bought by Persse, he had a forge in the yard – forge fire and bellows they did all the repairs on all the ploughs and harrows and all the implements and shod the horses.

There would be a man there everyday fulltime, and my grandfather had to do one day a week himself to make sure everything was running smooth.

PAULINE: *Did your grandfather go to a few big houses?*

It was he who organised the whole thing, my grandfather was very well-off. At that time he owned the forge in Ardrahan where Joyces are now, and he bought that house as well, he had a man in Cregclare and he had a man in Castletaylor, he had a lot of work that way. He made gates for farms and shod all the horses. Everyone nearly had one horse, so that time two neighbours join together and they would have a team of horses between them, they would plough and harrow and all the rest of it. The carpenter would made the common harrow and the fins had to be pointed and everything was made in the forge fire, I remember even during the war there was no welders, no drills, no electricity we only got electricity in Ardrahan, March 1948, Ardrahan was one of the first rural villages in Ireland to get rural electricity. I went into the business in 1952 and I bought an electric drill a big undertaking, bought a welder in 1952.

I shod horses as well as my father, shod 40 yearlings for a fair, people used breed horses and sell them at fairs, there would be horse fairs in Gort and Loughrea; before the fair young horses would be running around with their mothers, they would flock them put a rope halter and bring them in put 2 shoes on them two front shoes to make them look well. They would be very wild, no bit in their mouth they would rear up and kick you.

PAULINE: *How often would you shoe horses?*

Every month or 6 weeks or so depending sometimes they would pull shoes, if they were Clydesdale they would hold a shoe a lot longer but the Irish draft or half breed the shoes wouldn't be so strong. Clydesdale could hold a shoe for six months but you had an awful problem he had a big long hoof to take it off, the shoes would be worn some horses were shod 3–4 times a year.

PAULINE: *What did it cost to shoe horses?*

When I was shoeing horses – 14 shillings for 4 shoes. I will tell you a very good one. Take off the 4 shoes, pair the hooves, put them on again for 6 shillings, you took off the 4 shoes, put them in the fire and reshaped them, pared the hoof, put nails in each of them and you finished them off at 6 shillings. At a year and a half they came in out of the grass you put 2 old shoes on them, that was only 3 shillings, you could be an hour at that maybe 2, you put a rouch on them – that was a rope on their top lip, or used a tongs. You could do 8–10 horses a day and that would be hard work.

PAULINE: *What would happen if you didn't put shoes on horses?*

If you were doing a lot of road work they would get tender then get lame, their hooves would wear, that time there were no tar roads, by-roads with stones on the road some heavy horses would be very severe on shoes. One of the last horses I shod it was a mare, she was cracked because she was taken away from the foal, and she was very wild; I went out and she stood up on her hind legs – I put on the 2 shoes, 3 shillings – I was nearly as mad as the mare.

I was brought up with it since I could walk. We knew everything about nails different size nails for different size horses no. 9, nail no. 8 nail very popular no. 4, 5 or 6. Light hooves light nails – you had to drive the nail on the wall of the hoof if you were in too deep you would hurt them or poison them.

PAULINE: *Is there a difference between a blacksmith and a farrier?*

Well a farrier is completely shoeing horses only. A blacksmith does everything making tongs, gates, fixing ploughs, harrows everything anything in steel.

PAULINE: *Do you think it is a dying trade?*

Dying, you would get no-one to do iron work on the anvil or anything, it is all bought new. You made the gates and scrolls freehand. The forge fire we had no bellows, we had a blower, we bought it after the war £16 – it was a lot of money that time.

30 October 2002

I was born in Dublin, as I say, and I lived in Raheen for so-many years. I went to National school there, every day if it was fine, we could get out and we had two very severe teachers, one male and one female and they trounced us absolutely, all the kids.

PAULINE: *You went to a mixed school? I mean with Catholics?*

Yes, it was a Catholic school, there was nowhere else to go. There were about 40 or 50 Protestant families in the area, and they reduced since then. But we were slashed at school if we didn't know our lessons. I think there is a big difference now they are not allowed beat them or slash them. But I did not like school, then at 12 years of age I went away to Dublin to a boarding school and I stayed there for four years. I think I did my Junior, or my Inter, and when I came home my Aunt Annie, that lady you see there in the picture, she was very ill, and my father said, 'You might as well come now, you might as well look after your Aunt Annie', so I started in and nursed her for eleven years once I left school. Looked after her, did everything for her, used to bring her in a wheelchair to the fields – she was a farmer, you see, and she used to love to go up the fields to count the sheep and count the cattle and all this, you know? My home was only a mile away from there and I was over and back you know, and I could come home any night I wanted to, and come back in the morning, and she had a sister in the house who was a returned Yank, Aunt Jean.

PAULINE: *Was there no work for girls around that time or was it unusual to do what you did?*

There was no work in those days like there is now, no, no work at all like factories or like what they have now.

PAULINE: *So were you getting money for this?*

Not at all, didn't get a penny, but she was my aunt, you see, I got it later on, when I got married. I had five sisters and one brother, they all lived at home. They all went away to school.

PAULINE: *Was that unusual at the time?*

Oh they all went away to boarding school, anyone who could afford to send them.

PAULINE: *And what did your father do?*

My father was a farmer, and my mother was a clergyman's daughter, her father was the Dean of Clonfert, and that was a big diocese now, and everybody idolised him and he had a beautiful orchard, apples, peaches, pears, plums, everything. And this time of year Halloween, he'd always bring out baskets and baskets of fruit to the pump outside his door, and when the children would be coming down from school he had them there and he'd fire them down to them all. Dean Bradshaw.

PAULINE: *And what was your name before you got married?*

Taylor. And I married a Taylor. My mother's name was Bradshaw, she married Benjamin Taylor.

PAULINE: *Were they any relation to Shaw Taylor?*

No connection whatsoever. People think that, there's no connection.

PAULINE: *And where was Dick from?*

Dick was from Athenry, and where I met him, when Aunt Annie died, I went off to England nursing. And I was no sooner over there when I got septicaemia, and that's a very dangerous complaint, but I got through it, and then I came home – what did I do when I came home? I did two and a half years nursing in the Middlesex hospital in England.

PAULINE: *What year would that have been? 1930s would it have been?*

But – when I came home I was invited to Ardrahan on a holiday by Ellie Taylor, she was Dick's aunt. I knew her, I knew her very well, because she used to come to Kilchreest to Aunt Annie, they were always great friends, but I was invited by her, and I came over here, and who was here but Dick, into my barrow! [*laughs*]. Dick was living here, actually he was living in Ferndale at the time with his Aunt Margie and I met up with him you see, and sure Dick and I were going out walking the roads every day, and the next thing love got the better of us and we became great, and he proposed and the next thing we were engaged, and we were married. And I moved to Ardrahan and we moved into Ferndale.

PAULINE: *But Dick was left this place?*

Oh yes, he was left that by Uncle Ben. The old Ben, Ben Taylor, James, John, you probably heard of them. They were all 4 or 5 or 6 old men living together and Ben he owned the land, he owned all Cregclare, and he left all that to Dick, so Dick got that, so he farmed it, and made money on it, and he had the farm below the station.

PAULINE: *So you were wealthy farmers? And when did you start the dairy then?*

Well then you see somebody said, somebody wanted milk, we had cows you see, and I was churning, but that was all new to me, churning butter you know,but I got into it and I used to make over 30lb of butter a week, and it was no sooner made up than people were looking for it, that was the guards, the sergeant, and anybody that wanted a bit of butter and it was lovely butter, it was hard – then people would say, 'Mrs Taylor, would you sell me a pint of milk', you see, so out of that the dairy started, and I had more people coming in that door for milk – they would rise the window and take their bottle. A hundred bottles of milk in the end I was selling you know, that height of cream [*demonstrates*] on the top of the bottle – I don't know if you ever saw it

PAULINE: *I used to come down to get a bottle, that was towards the end of it now really.*

We were a good while in that and then selling a cow and buying another one.

PAULINE: *You never had any children?*

No, not really. I got used to it. I would have loved to have had, because I loved children, yeah, sure all the children used to be coming in to me. It was God's will. Dick used to say to me, as long as we are happy and in our health, he'd say, I don't mind.

PAULINE: *Were there many Protestants in Ardrahan when you came here?*

When I came here there were about 10 or 12 I think. There'd be Shaw Taylor, we have Taylors over there James and Ellie, John Henry the hotel as we call it, Dick and myself. We might have the odd straggler coming in from the country, but that's all that there was here at the time but you would get more you see, and then die off again.

PAULINE: *You never had any trouble with Catholics or vice versa?*

Not a bit in the slightest. Roman Catholics were our best friends and still are today. As children we would have played with them, then and now our best friends.

PAULINE: *Are many of your family alive?*

I have my eldest sister dead, Olive, my brother is dead, Dorothy and myself are alive, I am 88 and that is not bad, Ellis is 92, he is doing well,

PAULINE: *Had you many people working for you?*

We had 6 at one time, then it went to 5, and 4 in the end, and sort of cut down and it took something to pay them I can tell you when the wages went up, but they were good lads.

PAULINE: *J.J. and Mick Martyn, I remember them.*

Peter Linnane.

PAULINE: *So you have seen a lot of changes in Ardrahan?*

Well do you know it is the same village since I came into it. There is no improvement only those footpaths they have put in the street, they ruined the street by putting them there.

I'll tell you how we came by this house. You see that house over there was very big, my mother, she used to live with me quite a while. And she died with me, and there was an awful stairs up to her room from the kitchen, and that used to kill me absolutely. So I said to Dick, I was thinking of going to England for a wedding, and he said to me before I went, 'What would you like for Christmas?' 'Well I will tell you now', I said, 'Dick, and I mean this whole-heartedly, I'd love a bungalow and to get out of this big house, it's killing me'. He said, 'I thought that myself'. So I went to England and I was only a few days over there when I got a letter with the plans of the house, the whole thing for me to see. He said, 'you have your wish, I've booked an architect to look at the spot so we will build a bungalow in the orchard' – this was the old orchard. So I got my Christmas present, my bungalow. The old house was very big, big stairs up, go into the hall, and if a person was very ill and they had to go to the toilet, they had to leave the kitchen and go through the breakfast room and into the hall and turn around and to into another hall and up the stairs.

PAULINE: *Where did you get married?*

We got married in Loughrea Church, and the reception was in the Railway Hotel. There was 150 at it, a lot in those days. My father said you had a right to add another 10 or 20 to it, he said.

PAULINE: *Did you have a honeymoon?*

We went off out foreign, went to England and then to Spain.

PAULINE: *It was unusual that time wasn't it?*

No, oh, a lot of people used to do that, and we came home, and my dear, that was the time, wait now, there was a strike on at the time and there was no train, what was it – we couldn't get a train from Dublin to Cork, when we were coming home, and we stayed in Cork, and we went from that out to Tramore, 4 days there and we rang them up. Here we were coming home on such and such a night, got a bus to Kinvara, and hired a car, and the house was full outside, Nina from Athenry was up doing the catering and looking after things, that is Ellis's twin sister. So we went in, they got the land of their lives when they saw us, they were expecting us so long. But we had a grand time, we had a singsong for the night, went to bed and went on from that the next day.

PAULINE: *You would have been upper-class people would you?*

[*Laughing*] what do you mean?

PAULINE: *You would have been the wealthier people I suppose?*

I suppose you could say that, there was a lot of poverty around. But Daddy was a farmer.

PAULINE: *Had you many boyfriends before you met Dick?*

Oh one or two. I settled for Dick, he was a gentleman, a grand lad. He died when he was in his 80s, the Taylors are a very long-to-live family, I had an aunt who was 96 when she died, and she had an uncle who was 108, and there was another one they called him Faddy, I don't know why they called him Faddy, he was 114, their graves are beyond in Killina graveyard, and the date is on there. Over in Roxborough, it was one of my grandfather's churches. My grandfather was in the parish of Kilchreest, Killina, Loughrea and Moyode. He had all those churches to do and he was the dean of Clonfert. He had two daughters and a son, my mother and her sister Irene, Percy the son he joined the [British] army, Mother married Father and aunt Irene was working in Dublin. We had a pony and trap and a driver, he would come every Sunday morning and bring us to the church.

PAULINE: *You had a privileged childhood really compared to other people? Walking miles in bare feet.*

Well I tell you when I was going to school, we used to look forward to the fine weather coming after Christmas to throw off the shoes and walk to school in bare feet, now we used to love that, and come home with your toes broken.

PAULINE: *Did you have religion class in National school?*

No, not at school, we had religious instructions every week, the Dean came to our house. The school had religion hour or whatever it was every day and we were put out, it didn't matter if it were hail, rain or snow we had to go out, and we ate our lunch outside, we thought that was terrible, we had to go along with it, there was nothing we could do. There was something about that on the news recently, teaching both religions in one school, they don't want it as well, I think, but it could be done, because it is the one God we are all going to and there isn't much between the Roman Catholic and the Protestant religion.

PAULINE: *Were you the only [Protestant] family?*

No, the Glosters in Ballingarry, they were another family, so we would go out and sit on a cold rock. But when we got out into the yard and played, we were great friends with the other children.

PAULINE: *They wouldn't have wondered why you wouldn't have stayed in?*

No, they wouldn't have wondered, they just knew, I suppose they said to themselves, they must be out of the ordinary.

SADIE BERMINGHAM

Sadie didn't give an interview but recited this poem:

AN OLD WOMAN OF THE ROADS
Padraic Colum

O, to have a little house!
To own the hearth and stool and all!
The heaped up sods upon the fire,
The pile of turf against the wall!

To have a clock with weights and chains
And pendulum swinging up and down!
A dresser filled with shining delph,
Speckled and white and blue and brown!

I could be busy all the day
Clearing and sweeping hearth and floor,
And fixing on their shelf again
My blue and white and speckled store!

I could be quiet there at night
Beside the fire and by myself,
Sure of a bed and loth to leave
The ticking clock and the shining delph!

Och! But I'm weary of mist and dark,
And roads where there's never a house nor bush,
And tired I am of bog and road,
And the crying wind and the lonesome hush!

And I am praying to God on high,
And I am praying to Him night and day,
For a little house – a house of my own –
Out of the wind's and the rain's way.

ABOUT THE EDITOR

Pauline Bermingham Scully, BA, H.Dip, MA, is currently studying for a Diploma in Psychology and Counselling at Galway University. She was born in Ardrahan, County Galway and has lived there most of her life. She is currently working on a second volume of reminiscences for publication in December 2015.